PEOPLE
IN THE NEWS

The Osbournes

by Andy Koopmans

**LUCENT
BOOKS**®

THOMSON

™

GALE

San Diego • Detroit • New York • San Francisco • Cleveland
New Haven, Conn. • Waterville, Maine • London • Munich

To the Osbournes, particularly Ozzy, whose lasting dedication
to making music and pleasing his audience I greatly admire.

LIBRARY OF CONGRESS CATALOGING-IN-PUBLICATION DATA

Koopmans, Andy.
    The Osbournes / by Andy Koopmans.
        p. cm. — (People in the news)
    Summary: A biography of Ozzy Osbourne, a musician who toured with Black Sabbath
    and as a solo act, featuring the MTV reality television program filmed in the mansion
    he shares with wife Sharon and their two youngest children.
    Includes bibliographical references and index.
    ISBN 1-59018-451-3 (hardback : alk. paper)
    1. Osbournes (Television program)—Juvenile literature. 2. Osborne family—Juvenile
    literature. 3. Osbourne, Ozzy, 1948—Juvenile literature. [1. Osbournes (Television
    program) 2. Osborne family. 3. Osbourne, Ozzy, 1948– 4. Musicians. 5. Television
    personalities.] I. Title. II. People in the news (San Diego, Calif.)
    PN1992.77.O79K66 2004
    791.45'72—dc21
                                                                                2003006834

Printed in the United States of America

Table of Contents

Foreword

FAME AND CELEBRITY are alluring. People are drawn to those who walk in fame's spotlight, whether they are known for great accomplishments or for notorious deeds. The lives of the famous pique public interest and attract attention, perhaps because their experiences seem in some ways so different from, yet in other ways so similar to, our own.

Newspapers, magazines, and television regularly capitalize on this fascination with celebrity by running profiles of famous people. For example, television programs such as *Entertainment Tonight* devote all of their programming to stories about entertainment and entertainers. Magazines such as *People* fill their pages with stories of the private lives of famous people. Even newspapers, newsmagazines, and television news frequently delve into the lives of well-known personalities. Despite the number of articles and programs, few provide more than a superficial glimpse at their subjects.

Lucent's People in the News series offers young readers a deeper look into the lives of today's newsmakers, the influences that have shaped them, and the impact they have had in their fields of endeavor and on other people's lives. The subjects of the series hail from many disciplines and walks of life. They include authors, musicians, athletes, political leaders, entertainers, entrepreneurs, and others who have made a mark on modern life and who, in many cases, will continue to do so for years to come.

These biographies are more than factual chronicles. Each book emphasizes the contributions, accomplishments, or deeds that have brought fame or notoriety to the individual and shows how that person has influenced modern life. Authors portray their subjects in a realistic, unsentimental light. For example, Bill Gates—the cofounder and chief executive officer of the software giant Microsoft—has been instrumental in making personal computers the most vital tool of the modern age. Few dispute his business savvy, his perseverance, or his technical expertise, yet critics say he is ruthless in his dealings with competitors and driven more by his desire to maintain Microsoft's dominance in the computer industry than by an interest in furthering technology.

In these books, young readers will encounter inspiring stories about real people who achieved success despite enormous obstacles. Oprah Winfrey—the most powerful, most watched, and wealthiest woman on television today—spent the first six years of her life in the care of her grandparents while her unwed mother sought work and a better life elsewhere. Her adolescence was colored by promiscuity, pregnancy at age fourteen, rape, and sexual abuse.

Each author documents and supports his or her work with an array of primary and secondary source quotations taken from diaries, letters, speeches, and interviews. All quotes are footnoted to show readers exactly how and where biographers derive their information and provide guidance for further research. The quotations enliven the text by giving readers eyewitness views of the life and accomplishments of each person covered in the People in the News series.

In addition, each book in the series includes photographs, annotated bibliographies, timelines, and comprehensive indexes. For both the casual reader and the student researcher, the People in the News series offers insight into the lives of today's newsmakers—people who shape the way we live, work, and play in the modern age.

Introduction

Osbourne Family Values

IN MARCH 2002, the MTV network premiered its new cable program *The Osbournes,* an unscripted "reality" program featuring the day-to-day life of rock star Ozzy Osbourne, his wife Sharon, and their children Kelly and Jack. Before its debut, few people at the network or in the Osbourne family expected the show to become one of the highest rated cable programs in history. But it did. More viewers tuned in to watch the first and second seasons of *The Osbournes* than did for the leading HBO drama *The Sopranos* or the long-running popular news program *Meet the Press.*

Many critics and entertainment industry executives have tried to understand the show's popularity. Ozzy Osbourne, whose music career began in the late 1960s, had, by the late 1990s, been called washed-up and a has-been by many in the music industry. As reporter Ed Masley of the *Pittsburgh Post-Gazette* wrote, in 1991, Osbourne was "written off as bound for the dinosaur graveyard in the Rolling Stone Album Guide."[1]

Nonetheless, after *The Osbournes* debuted, millions of viewers in North America and the United Kingdom tuned in each week to watch the family go about their simultaneously unusual and ordinary lives. The family was certainly unusual—not many households are headed by the self-proclaimed Prince of Darkness of rock (Ozzy) and one of the toughest business managers in music (Sharon). Viewers saw from the beginning that this family was unconventional: For instance, on the day the family moved into their Beverly Hills mansion, amid ordinary belongings like linens and furniture, movers also brought in boxes marked "Crucifixes,"

"Dead Things," and "Devil's Heads." Additionally, cussing is a regular part of the Osbourne vocabulary and is tolerated by all in the Osbourne household. The family kept MTV network censors busy "bleeping" the frequent profanity out of the broadcast.

However, many people attribute the show's popularity to the fact that it revealed the Osbournes to be in many ways a very normal family. It showed that despite their eccentricities, celebrity, and wealth, the family had to deal with similar day-to-day life issues as many other families, such as parents instructing children about drinking and drugs, arguments between siblings, and how to deal with incontinent and destructive household pets. Many people particularly responded to the fact that, in spite of the frequent loud arguments laced with profanity, the family members demonstrated strong commitment and love toward each other. As psychologist John Light explains, "There's love in this family; that's why people like (the show)."[2]

The enormously popular MTV show The Osbournes *offers viewers a glimpse of the daily lives of (left to right) Ozzy, Sharon, Kelly, and Jack Osbourne.*

Another critic, Alessandra Stanley, said that Ozzy Osbourne's life seemed almost as if it were made for television: "Ozzy's life is so fictional. It's as if someone created this loony heavy metal star from England who settles in Beverly Hills. But it's real life, so it can't succumb to the icky conventions of sitcoms."[3]

Whatever the reason for the show's popularity, *The Osbournes* has become an extremely popular cultural phenomenon, complete with accessories. *The Osbournes* T-shirts, posters, mugs, and action figures have sold very well. There is even a Sony PlayStation 2 video game, *Black Skies,* based on Ozzy Osbourne.

The popularity of the show and merchandising have made the Osbournes—who were already multimillionaires—one of the top-earning celebrity families. The family, with an estimated fortune worth $124 million in 2003, owns two houses—a $17 million house in Buckinghamshire, England, and the $10 million mansion in Beverly Hills, where the show's first two seasons were filmed. According to Britain's *Heat* magazine, with the proceeds of their show, *The Osbournes* merchandise, and other entertainment business projects, as a family, the Osbournes were the third-highest-earning celebrities in the UK, making more than $60 million in 2002 alone.

The Osbourne empire continues to grow, paving the way for the Osbourne childrens' careers in show business, and for numerous other opportunities for every member of the family. Although Ozzy Osbourne has repeatedly said that he would be dead, broke, or both without his wife Sharon Osbourne, the phenomenon that is *The Osbournes* has Ozzy Osbourne himself as its foundation. His story begins in England, just after the end of World War II.

Chapter 1

Ozzy: The Escape

B ORN INTO THE bleak atmosphere of working-class England in the years immediately following World War II, Ozzy Osbourne spent his youth seeking a way to escape his surroundings. From his childhood through his young adulthood, Osbourne turned to whatever distraction or avenue of escape he could find to get away from the harsh reality of his life, including the fantasy of television, the delirium of drugs and alcohol, and even attempted suicide. However, it was music that finally provided his escape.

Hard Times

Ozzy Osbourne was born John Michael Osbourne on December 3, 1948, in Aston, a low-income industrial section of Birmingham, England. Ozzy was the fourth child of six born to John Osbourne Sr., called "Jack," and Lillian Osbourne. Jack and Lillian Osbourne were blue-collar workers: Jack worked the night shift as a machinist at the GEC metals factory in nearby Whitton, while Lillian worked the day shift at the Lucas automobile assembly plant in Aston.

During the years following World War II, life in much of England, and particularly places like Aston, was difficult because of the hardships caused by years of bombings during the war. Even in the years after the war, food rationing was still in place and material goods were scarce. It was especially difficult for many working-class people, Osbourne's parents among them, to make enough money to provide a good life for themselves and their families.

Although Jack and Lillian worked long hours, their jobs did not pay well, and, consequently, the family struggled to get by. The family of eight shared a two-bedroom house at 14 Lodge Road, amid rows upon rows of other homes just like it. The house

Osbourne poses with his mother Lillian (second from right) at his wedding. Although both his father and mother worked long hours, the family had trouble making ends meet.

was small and had only one toilet, which was outdoors in the small, concrete-slab backyard. Osbourne recalled living in the crowded conditions:

> It's unbelievable that the six of us kids plus me mum and dad could live in a place no bigger than the Queen Vic bar. We had two bedrooms and an annexe. Me and my brother used to share the same bed. As the older ones got married and moved out, the oldest one left got the annexe room."[4]

Troubled Home Life

The Osbourne household was not often a happy one. Osbourne's father regularly arrived home from work drunk, having stopped at the local pub along the way, and frequent arguments broke out between him and Lillian. Often, the arguments turned violent, and Osbourne's father would beat his wife. The reason for the fights was usually the family's lack of money. Although Jack and Lillian never let their children go without the essentials of food and clothing, Osbourne recalls that for many years he only had one set of clothes to wear: "I had one pair of socks, never wore underwear, one pair of pants and one jacket—and that was it."[5]

As a child, Osbourne lived in this house in Aston, Birmingham, England. Osbourne had a very difficult childhood.

Osbourne recalled that the poverty and troubles at home, coupled with the generally bleak atmosphere of Aston, depressed him and often made life seem hopeless. From the time he was very young, Osbourne wanted to escape the poverty and surroundings of his hometown. He vowed to someday get himself and his family out of there. As Osbourne remembered:

> My father and [mother were] always fighting over something. And I used to sit on the front steps all the time and think, "One of these days I'm going to buy a Rolls Royce and drive them out of this [place]."[6]

School Days

From his first years in school, it was clear that academics were not going to be Osbourne's way out of Aston. Osbourne—nicknamed "Ozzy" by his classmates—was a poor student. Later, as an adult, doctors diagnosed him with dyslexia and attention deficit disorder, but such conditions were not recognized or even heard of in those days. Instead of offering him assistance, his teachers simply presumed he was dumb because he did not read well or pay attention to his work. He said: "I used to . . . get in trouble a lot because I would stare at the blackboard and I wouldn't understand what the teacher was writing. . . . It just didn't make sense, like writing in Chinese."[7]

Although he did poorly in class, Osbourne developed a love of entertaining people during his school years. He had learned the value of entertainment as escape early on. One of the few luxuries Osbourne's parents were able to afford was a television, which Osbourne watched as much as possible to get away from the reality of his life. His favorite shows included *I Love Lucy, Lassie,* and *Roy Rogers.* Additionally, in school, he tried to entertain fellow students. He loved to make people laugh by throwing himself around, hitting himself in the head, or pretending to trip and fall.

Wild Child

Osbourne's childhood and adolescence were difficult for him. He hated school, was troubled by persistent money problems at home, and was generally confused and depressed much of the time. He acted out, often violently. When he was eleven years old, he stabbed his aunt's cat, and once he tried to set his older sister on fire. As an adolescent in school, he organized "hanging squads" in which he and a few other friends would force kids into bathrooms or other places and hang them until they nearly strangulated. Then, when he was fourteen years old, Osbourne tried to hang himself. He made a noose out of his mother's clothesline, put it around his neck, and tied the other end to a high gate. He jumped off a chair to strangle himself but his father caught him in the act and cut him down. His father was so angry with Osbourne that he gave him a beating as punishment.

Osbourne also regularly got into trouble for ditching classes. He spent time in cafes with his friends and played pool in local pool halls. Osbourne also began drinking and taking various drugs to escape reality when he was young, habits that would trouble him later and persist for nearly thirty years. His father was a heavy drinker, and Osbourne learned by example, taking his first drink—beer mixed with lemonade—at twelve years old at a pub with his father. At first he did not like the taste, but he learned to enjoy its effects. He remembered: "When I drank my first pint, I thought, 'This can't be what my dad drinks! It's revolting!' But then I got this warm feeling and I thought, 'Maybe it is.'"[8]

Drugs were also an easy means of escape and were readily available. Osbourne began smoking marijuana and taking whatever pharmaceutical pills he could get his hands on when he was in his early teens. He frequently stayed up all night taking amphetamines and drinking beer or smoking marijuana. He also started smoking cigarettes, a habit that would last nearly forty years.

The Influence of Music

Although there were many negative influences in Osbourne's youth, there was also a significant positive influence—music. Music was an important form of entertainment in the Osbourne household, as his mother often sang and his family frequently joined in sing-alongs to pass the time. Because of these experiences, Osbourne developed his singing ability. He even began performing in school productions, such as the musicals *HMS Pinafore, Pirates of Penzance,* and *The Mikado.*

Osbourne's sisters also introduced him to rock and roll when he was young. They brought home albums by musicians such as Chuck Berry, and Osbourne would dance and sing to the music. However, the group that made him decide to try to become a musician was the Beatles, a group of four working-class young men from Liverpool, England, an industrial town much like Birmingham. Osbourne first heard the Beatles' single "She Loves You" when it was released in 1961 and he fell in love with the music. He remembered: "'She Loves You' was the first record I ever bought. . . . It changed everything."[9]

Osbourne collected all of the Beatles' singles as they came out, taking part-time jobs, such as newspaper routes and grocery bagging, for the money to buy them. When he did not have the money, he would shoplift the records. He learned the songs by heart and sang them throughout the day. "I thought being a Beatle would be a great way to get out of Birmingham," he said later. "I used to dream that [Beatle] Paul McCartney would marry my sister. That was going to be my ticket into the Beatles. Unfortunately, Paul wouldn't have liked my sister."[10]

The Beatles (left to right, Paul McCartney, Ringo Starr, George Harrison, and John Lennon) were a major musical influence on the young Osbourne.

Slaughterhouse Blues

Ozzy Osbourne worked at a number of menial labor jobs as a young man after quitting school. Among them was a job working at a slaughterhouse. In Harry Shaw's book *Ozzy "Talking,"* Osbourne, who became a vegetarian in the late 1990s, remembers the disgusting conditions of the job:

> There was a giant mountain of sheep's stomachs . . . and my job was to get this knife and cut them up and empty the [contents] out of the stomachs. I was so tired of throwing up, my eyes were bulging out of my head from straining. Everyone who eats meat should walk through an abattoir [slaughterhouse]. You will not make four steps without puking your guts out. I guarantee.

In spite of his love of music and strong desire to be a musician, the practical necessity for money, and his father's insistence that he learn a trade, convinced Osbourne that he should become a plumber. Plumbing was a respectable trade that made a good wage, which he thought he could use to help contribute to the family's income and alleviate some of the arguments and problems between his parents. School was like prison to Osbourne, so he dropped out for good at the earliest age allowed—fifteen years old—to become a plumber's apprentice. In this position, he would assist a working plumber for several years in order to learn the trade.

Odd Jobs

The plumber's apprenticeship did not last long. Apprenticeship was hard work for low pay and Osbourne quit after a few months. While the English economy had picked up by the early 1960s and there were many jobs available, Osbourne was young and unskilled, thus he could find only menial, unpleasant work. He had a series of odd jobs, including working in a mortuary, a slaughterhouse, and tuning car horns at the same car assembly factory where his mother worked. He felt that the jobs were dead ends, and he did not want to end up like his father or the other men who worked in the factories. He recalled,

> When I worked at Lucas tuning car horns I remember saying to this guy Harry, how long have you been working here? And he got all proud of himself, "35 years come this summer, and I get this gold watch when I retire," [he

said]. I thought if I want a . . . gold watch that bad, I'll go and break a jeweler's window and run off with one."[11]

Crime Does Not Pay for Ozzy

Osbourne decided that it would be easier to steal than to work for money. At seventeen years old, he started burglarizing shops, boardinghouses, and a clothing store behind his house. However, Osbourne was a comically bad burglar. He knew from watching television and movies that burglars wore gloves when they worked, but did not realize it was to guard against leaving fingerprints. He used a pair of fingerless gloves, leaving his fingerprints all over the scenes of his crimes. He once escaped from one burglary by climbing over a wall while carrying a large television set. He lost his balance and fell, and the television landed on top of him. Police finally caught Osbourne when he returned to rob a clothing store behind his house for a second time. The court charged Osbourne with burglary (breaking in), larceny (stealing personal goods), assault (for resisting arrest), and possession of a small amount of marijuana, which he was carrying with him. Although the court was lenient and sentenced him with only a fine, he still had to serve three months in jail because he could not afford to pay the money.

Later, Osbourne would reflect that although jail scared him, it was not all bad because he got along well with most of the other prisoners and he got free food and cigarettes. For him, the boredom was the worst part of jail. Prisoners spent only two hours a day outside their cells. To pass the time, Osbourne gave himself tattoos using a sewing needle and a tin of metal polish. He gave himself the prominent O-Z-Z-Y tattoo on the fingers of his left hand, and he also tattooed a smiley face on each of his knees so that he would have something cheerful to look at each morning when he woke up in prison.

Reformed

When Osbourne got out of jail, he decided that he had to put crime behind him and try to do something else to avoid going back. At seventeen, he tried to join the British army thinking it would please his father, but the recruiter rejected Osbourne because of his unusual appearance. He remembered, "I had a [beer] tap around my neck on a string for jewelry, I was wearing a pyjama top, and my backside was hanging out." [12]

An army reject, an incompetent criminal, and disgusted by the jobs he gould get, Osbourne looked around for something else to do. The one thing that still interested him was music. In the time since he had first started listening to the Beatles, they had become the most popular band in the world. He thought, if four Liverpool boys could become world famous, then so could he.

Osbourne shows off the O-Z-Z-Y tattoo he gave himself at age seventeen while in jail. His experience in prison caused him to give up his life of crime.

Osbourne had never learned to play an instrument because he was not allowed to practice in the house. His father worked nights and the noise would have interrupted his father's daytime sleep. However, Osbourne could sing and he felt that would be enough.

Jack Osbourne was skeptical about his son's interest in music, thinking it would be difficult to make a living in a band. With Osbourne's troubled background, he worried about Ozzy. Osbourne remembered: "My father said I'd end up either in prison or [being] something special. I love my father. I wanted to achieve something for him because my grades in school were bad." [13]

New Direction

Despite his concerns about his son, Jack Osbourne recognized how much his son wanted to be a musician. He borrowed money to buy him a microphone and an amplifier for $50, equipment Osbourne needed to be heard over the other instruments in a rock band. Osbourne gratefully accepted the gift. He then came up with a stage name for himself, Ozzy Zigg, and put up a flyer in local music stores advertising himself as a singer in need of a band.

Osbourne briefly played with two bands. A school friend started the first band, Approach. They rehearsed and played in numerous places—old garages, empty movie theaters, and wherever they could find spare room. The sound of his voice over the amplifier amazed and pleased Osbourne. He knew he had a talent and was eager for more people to hear him. Feeling that Approach would never become much of a band, he quit and joined another band called Music Machine, which regularly performed small gigs around Birmingham. However, Music Machine split up after a few frustrating months of struggling unsuccessfully to work their way into larger venues.

Then, in 1967, another local musician named Terrence Butler, nicknamed "Geezer," answered Osbourne's ad. Butler had been playing guitar for only a few months, but Osbourne and Butler decided to start their own band, calling themselves Rare Breed.

Earth

Meanwhile, one of Osbourne's former schoolmates, a guitarist named Tony Iommi, had started a band called Mythology with a

Osbourne (far right) teamed up with (left to right) Geezer Butler, Tony Iommi, and Bill Ward in 1967 to form a band called Earth.

drummer named William (Bill) Ward and singer Chris Smith. Mythology moved out of Birmingham to a town named Carlisle, near the border of England and Scotland. They became popular playing covers of blues songs. Although they had a good number of fans, the band split up and moved back to Birmingham.

Iommi and Ward decided to re-form a band but they needed a singer. Iommi saw Osbourne's advertisement and decided to meet him. In school, Iommi and Osbourne had known and disliked each other. In fact, Iommi had frequently beaten up on Osbourne, who was not much of a fighter. Iommi had also heard Osbourne sing in the school musicals and did not like his voice, so he hoped that the Ozzy Zigg of the ad was not Osbourne. When Iommi discovered it was, he refused to hire him. However, Osbourne and Butler offered Ward the position of drummer in their band Rare Breed. Ward agreed to join, but only if Iommi could join as well. So, despite their former dislike for each other, Iommi and Osbourne, along with Ward and Butler, began a new band together, which they called Earth. With Osbourne on vocals, Iommi on guitar, Butler on bass, and Ward on drums, the group played primarily covers of jazz and blues tunes.

The jazz and blues music did not fit the band well. They wanted to do something new and were drawn to rock, so they began to write their own music and experimented with new styles. Osbourne and the others did not like the trends in late-1960s popular music (other than the Beatles), which was heavily influenced by the hippie youth movement of the period and which did not reflect their feelings or where they came from. Instead, they developed songs that were harder and louder than the popular music they heard, with crashing drumbeats, loud guitar riffs, and dark and often angry lyrics. Osbourne later recalled:

> We got sick and tired of all the . . . love your brother and flower-power forever. We're just ordinary backstreet guys and we're just making a sound which is free suburban rock, if you like. Slum rock. The music we developed was loud and it was furious because that's exactly the way we felt at the time. [14]

Run-Ins with Satanists

Because Osbourne and his band mates renamed their band Black Sabbath, many people, including many Satanists, presumed the band was involved with the occult and black magic. In her book *Diary of a Madman: Ozzy Osbourne: The Stories Behind the Songs,* writer Carol Clerk describes how Osbourne reacted to some of these misunderstandings:

> Back in [the group's] early days, there was an endearing naivete about Ozzy in particular, who seemed genuinely bewildered at the extreme reactions that Sabbath provoked. "I remember when we started getting invites to black masses," he said. "We all looked at each other and said, 'Is this for real or what?'" . . .
>
> In Memphis too, . . . they found their dressing room walls smeared with crosses of blood, and where one deranged character sprang onto the stage brandishing a sacrificial knife. . . . Later, a crowd of people—said to be the local coven [a group of witches]—assembled outside their hotel. . . . Ozzy recalled: "I went to my hotel room. There were about 15 freaks outside my door with black-painted faces and robes and daggers and candles. I slammed the door and phoned the roadie. I said, 'There are a load of cuckoo brains out there.'"

Starting Out

In the late 1960s, there were hundreds of small bands playing all over England, all trying to achieve the same fame and success as the Beatles. Very few succeeded; most played whenever they could for little or no money and often to very small crowds. At first, such was the case with Osbourne's band. Earth played small gigs around Birmingham without gathering much of a following until they met Jim Simpson.

Simpson was a jazz musician and the owner of Henry's Blueshouse. His club had become extremely popular, and several bands that would go on to fame, including Led Zeppelin, played there. In 1968, the members of Earth approached Simpson to audition, and to see if he was interested in managing their band. Although Simpson did not think the band was technically very good, he liked Osbourne's singing and agreed to both propositions. Simpson arranged for Earth to open for one of the most popular club bands at the time, Ten Years After. Musicians in the audience liked Earth's performance and arranged for other gigs for the group, including one in London.

Although they were beginning to get work, the band was not making much money and the four men struggled to get by. According to Osbourne, at one point they were so poor that he and Ward shared one pair of shoes, taking turns going outside in them. The band got some financial support from Iommi's mother, who frequently fed them and lent them money and the use of her van to transport their equipment to performances. Nonetheless, the band was inspired to work hard at rehearsal, aware that they were in competition with several other bands that were receiving local attention, including the soon-to-be-popular Jethro Tull.

Becoming Black Sabbath

The group struggled through their first two years of existence, taking gigs wherever they could and often substituting for other bands who did not show up for performances. In 1968, when the band discovered that another group was also called Earth, they decided to change their name to avoid confusion. One day while waiting to rehearse, Iommi saw a poster for the 1963 Boris Karloff horror film *Black Sabbath* and remarked to his band mates that it was interesting that people would pay money to be scared. It was an inspiration: The band decided that if people would pay to see scary movies, they might pay to listen to scary music. They decided to write a song inspired by the idea and called it "Black Sabbath." Iommi came up with a guitar riff which, Osbourne said at the time, was "the scariest riff I've ever heard in my life."[15] The band changed its name to Black Sabbath and continued to innovate and experiment with their music, coming up with a style of loud, dark, and often "scary" music, which was eventually called heavy metal.

In spite of their innovations and hard work rehearsing, audiences frequently did not pay attention to the band when they played at clubs. People often talked through the performances. Osbourne tried to shock audiences to get a response. For one performance, he painted his face, hands, and feet purple. The trick did not work, however, and it took him weeks to remove the paint from his body. The band tried other strategies, such as increasing the volume level louder and louder until conversation was impossible and the audience had to listen.

The band continued to take whatever performances they could get, often performing for few people at small venues, but in early 1969 they got the opportunity to play a series of shows at the Star Club in Hamburg, Germany. The club had once hosted the Beatles for several months early in their career, and for Osbourne to follow the example of his idols was a great opportunity. The band was a huge success, playing seven shows a day and breaking attendance records set in the early 1960s by the Beatles themselves.

The First Album

After their return from Germany, the popularity of the band continued to grow and they decided that they had enough of a following and enough material to record an album. Through Jim Simpson, they found an independent record producer named Tony Hall, who paid the band to record a demo album at the London-based Regent Sound studio. Among the songs on the demo record were "Evil Woman" and "Rebel." They recorded the entire album in only eight hours, which was fast by the standards of most music recording of the time. Producing the record cost just six hundred pounds (U.S. $870).

Black Sabbath drew even larger crowds at the Star Club in Hamburg, Germany, than the Beatles.

Simpson managed the sale of the album, titled *Black Sabbath*. He took it to fourteen record companies before Vertigo Records accepted it. Although the band did not want to encourage associations between Black Sabbath and the occult, the record company thought the album would sell better if the band's image was depicted as Satanist and occult. Therefore, Vertigo insisted that the album's inside cover depict an upside-down cross. Further, the company released the album on Friday the thirteenth (of February 1970), a day often associated with black magic.

Hit Record

Despite the necessary compromises with the record label, Osbourne was excited and proud of the album. He took the record home to play for his parents to show them he had made something of himself. However, the music was not the kind his parents listened to. The lyrics were poetic but unusual, and the music was influenced by blues and the new "metal" sound, with loud electric

Critical Sabbath

Although the band would grow to become one of the most popular bands in the world, when they first started out, Black Sabbath rarely received good reviews from music critics. In his book *Ozzy "Talking,"* Harry Shaw quotes Ozzy Osbourne's opinion of the critics who wrote about the group in the late 1960s and early 1970s.

> To be quite honest, I've lived with the press slagging us off for such a long time, I'm quite used to it. Everyone's got their own opinion. It's them out there that matter to me. I'm not just doing it for the press. Nobody likes a bad slam. After you've been working all your merry hours in the studio, nobody likes a stab in the back from the press, but I suppose they're critics and if they weren't critics they wouldn't criticise. That's their job to knock a few holes in things. . . .

> For a time I did my damnedest to make [the critics] happy, but they took the [energy] out of me for that. They must think we're dumb. But a lot of people who were writing these things about Sabbath aren't reporting ten years later. They're sweeping the streets or they're doormen at some poxy club somewhere.

guitar riffs and crashing drumbeats. Osbourne's parents knew that the group often sat around drinking beer while writing and rehearsing their songs. After listening to the album, Osbourne's father looked at his son, puzzled, and asked, "Son, are you sure you're just drinking the occasional beer?" [16]

Although his parents' reaction was not what he had hoped, Osbourne could not help but be proud. The 105 pounds he received from the producer seemed like a fortune. "I'd never owned 100 quid in my life! I thought . . . I've won! I bought a bottle of Brut cologne, I gave my mum 30 quid and I got drunk on the rest." [17]

The album made the music charts in both the UK and the United States, reaching no. 8 and no. 23, respectively. The immediate popularity of the album in the UK was such that the band broke attendance records at Simpson's club when they performed.

The record company set up a tour for the album that included England, France, Germany, Belgium, the Netherlands, and the United States. The tour began immediately after the album was released, and by summer 1970, Black Sabbath was performing before a huge crowd in New York City. At twenty-one years old, Ozzy Osbourne had finally escaped.

Chapter 2

Ozzy: Let the Madness Begin

W HEN OZZY OSBOURNE and the other members of Black Sabbath went on tour for their first album, *Black Sabbath,* in 1970, they were almost unknown. They were all working-class men in their twenties, and Osbourne had rarely been outside Birmingham, and never outside of Europe. On the band's tour, Osbourne began what would became a decades-long career of fame and wealth; however, he was unprepared for the adulation and the lifestyle of a world-famous rock star.

In the early 1970s, Black Sabbath not only helped form a new genre of rock music, which would eventually become known as heavy metal, but they also became heavily involved in drugs, alcohol, and casual sex with female fans. For Osbourne, being a rock star was exciting and enjoyable, and he indulged his self-acknowledged addictive personality to the fullest. Over the next several years, however, the excesses of his lifestyle became detrimental to his personal life. His addictions were responsible for the breakup of his first marriage, for being fired from Black Sabbath, and for several physical and psychological breakdowns.

Rock-and-Roll Lifestyle

The 1970 European and American tour for their debut album was the beginning of five years of intensive recording and touring for Black Sabbath. During their Black Sabbath tour, they developed a following, especially in the United States. Their first appearance in America was in New York in October 1970, and Americans had never heard anything like their music. Determined

25

to make a significant first impression, Bill Ward threw his drum set into the audience at one point during the show. The crowd responded well, liking the aggression and wildness of Black Sabbath. The band did seven encores that night.

The four young musicians were completely unprepared for what it was like to tour in the United States. Osbourne and the other members of the band were suddenly surrounded by throngs of young female fans and people offering them drugs. As Osbourne remembered, "Touring America in the early seventies as a big success meant we had people throwing drugs at us all the time." [18]

Within a few years of the release of their debut album in 1970, Black Sabbath became one of the biggest bands in the world.

To the Top

The band's fame and wealth grew tremendously from 1970 to 1975, during which time they recorded another five albums in close succession, all of which sold millions of copies and achieved high rankings on the British and American music charts. The albums were *Paranoid* (1970), *Master of Reality* (1971), *Black Sabbath Volume 4* (1972), *Sabbath, Bloody Sabbath* (1973), and *Sabotage* (1975). By the mid-1970s, Black Sabbath was one of the most popular and famous bands in the world.

Critics, however, hated Black Sabbath, and parents thought they were a dangerous influence because of their occult image, their loud music, and the dark, strange lyrics of their songs. Nonetheless, Black Sabbath sold out enormous concert venues all over Europe and the United States. They were part of a new movement in rock, along with popular bands such as Led Zepplin and Deep Purple, who played "heavy" rock, distinguished by its loud, screeching guitars and smashing drums wielded by long-haired young men.

The band indulged fully in the rock-and-roll lifestyle of drugs, money, and sex. Osbourne was the most indulgent in all areas. He bought a castle in the wealthy Staffordshire area of England, collecting guns and expensive cars. On and off the road, he drank a lot, took as many drugs as he could get his hands on, and slept with many women. He said about his excessive behavior:

> I'm something of a madman. I can do nothing in moderation. If it's booze, I drink the place dry. If it's drugs, I take everything and then scrape the carpet for little crumbs. [19]

Thelma

Osbourne's drinking, drug use, and philandering also led to the destruction of his first marriage. In 1971, Osbourne married Thelma Mayfair, a woman he knew from Birmingham. Mayfair was a young, single mother with a five-year-old son named Elliott, whom Osbourne adopted after the wedding. The couple went on to have two children together, a daughter named Jessica Starshine, born in 1972, and a son named Louis, born in 1975.

Black Sabbath manager Jim Simpson said that Osbourne's relationship with Thelma Mayfair started out strong but deteriorated as Black Sabbath became increasingly famous. He said, "When they first met Ozzy was 18 and broke. But once he hit the big time, he undoubtedly changed and it was very difficult for Thelma to handle. . . . She was stuck at home with [three] young kids while her husband was touring the world and living it up."[20]

Osbourne later admitted that he was not a good husband to Mayfair or a good father to their children. He later said, "I got married to my first wife too young. I was a very abusive husband. I was a married bachelor, really."[21]

Aside from the numerous extramarital sexual relationships with women during his tours, Osbourne was gone most of the first years

of their marriage. When he was home, he was physically abusive toward his wife and had an unpredictable temper. For example, in 1975, he returned home from touring, emotionally and physically exhausted from many months of performing and drug bingeing. When Thelma Osbourne asked him to go out and feed the chickens they kept at their Staffordshire farm, Osbourne became furious. He grabbed a shotgun, went into the yard and shot all of the chickens. When the last one would not die, he grabbed a sword from the house and chased the bird around the yard until he saw he was being watched. He said:

Osbourne embraced the wild and indulgent life of a rock star on the road.

"I was stopped by the sight of my very respectable neighbour looking at me over the fence. 'Unwinding again, John?' she said."[22]

Breaking Down

Osbourne's unpredictable behavior was in part due to his tendency toward depression. Since he was a child, Osbourne had suffered from depression, and the condition remained a part of his personality as an adult. For Osbourne, frequently the only remedy for the blues was the one he had used as a teenager—acting out. Osbourne often played pranks, such as setting a man's newspaper on fire in an airport while he was reading it and sneaking into the tour bus at night to shave the eyebrows off sleeping crew members. He also destroyed hotel rooms and instruments. More seriously, though, Osbourne medicated his depression and boredom with yet more alcohol and drugs. However, while the substances alleviated his troubles during the highs, they inevitably made the low times worse. By the mid-1970s, Osbourne was drinking and taking drugs from the time he awoke in the morning to the time he went to bed at night, just to make it through the day. According to Osbourne:

> My day consisted of getting up, getting myself a drink as soon as possible, going straight down the pub at opening time, staying there all day, and taking more and more coke to keep me going. . . . Eventually I was in a terrible state; I couldn't eat, I couldn't sleep, I couldn't even control my own body—nothing. That's when I decided I was definitely going . . . mad.[23]

In 1977, Thelma Osbourne admitted him to a mental hospital after finding him driving one of his sports cars in circles all night in a field near their house. Hating the clinic, Osbourne checked himself back out immediately. Later in the year, however, he had another nervous collapse. After a day of bingeing on drugs, he killed all seventeen of the family cats with a shotgun and knife. Thelma Osbourne returned home to find Osbourne lying, covered in blood, underneath the piano. This time he checked himself into the mental hospital. However, he again left almost immediately, returning home to take some more cocaine.

Osbourne's lifestyle put a tremendous strain on his marriage. Osbourne rarely showed up at home and when he did, he was drunk and abusive. Tired of his behavior, Thelma Osbourne kicked her husband out of the house, leaving his possessions on the front lawn. Although Osbourne was upset, he understood that he had behaved badly in the marriage and he did not fight the separation. Osbourne lived away from his wife and family for the next several years.

Trouble at Work

At the same time that Osbourne's personal life was suffering, his career was having problems too. Infighting among the members of the band occurred regularly. While they had established a bond over their years of performing, their personalities often conflicted. Fights frequently broke out, particularly between Tony Iommi and Osbourne, who had never become close friends, despite being in a band together for several years.

Additionally, the excesses of the band's spending on material goods and drugs had severely cut into their profits. The band spent the money as fast as they made it and found themselves nearly broke, even when they had become world-famous rock stars.

The band also had several legal problems. In 1970, the band had fired Jim Simpson as their manager to work with more experienced managers Patrick Meehan and Wilf Pine. Simpson retaliated by suing the band for wrongful termination of their contract. The band spent the next several years dealing with the lawsuit, which ended up taking a large portion of the band's royalties.

The new management, however, also created problems for Black Sabbath. Under Meehan and Pine, the band benefited from all the trappings of wealth. Their managers provided anything they wanted, including large houses and expensive cars. However, unbeknownst to the band, all these things were not purchased from the money the band was making. Instead, they were owned by the managers who were paying themselves large salaries. The band, in fact, owned almost nothing and received almost none of the proceeds from their albums. The managers also took advantage of the inexperience of the band in the music business, paying the musicians meager salaries for their performances. For instance, in 1974, the band played at a concert called Cal Jam in Ontario, Canada, and each band member received one thousand dollars for the performance. The band later discovered that Meehan and Pine charged the promoters of the concert $250,000 for Black Sabbath's performance and had kept all but four thousand dollars for themselves. The band fired Meehan and Pine over this dispute in 1975. To the band's surprise, when they left, the managers took back all of the material possessions that the band assumed they owned, leaving Black Sabbath nearly broke.

Frustrated by their management experiences, Osbourne and the other band members decided to manage Black Sabbath on their own. However, managing one of the world's most popular bands was not easy, particularly when all of the musicians were regularly intoxicated. Recognizing they needed a professional, in 1976, Black Sabbath hired Don Arden, the president of Jet Records, as their manager.

Called "the Godfather" by many in the music business, Don Arden was a former singer and entertainer who had become a well-known manager and promoter with a reputation for being a tough and able businessman. He was one of the first people to bring American popular music to England. He represented numerous renowned groups, such as The Move and the Electric Light Orchestra (ELO). He was also the father of Sharon Arden, who years later would become Osbourne's wife.

Black Sabbath hired Don Arden, father of Osbourne's future wife, Sharon, as their manager in 1976.

Professional and Personal Trouble

In 1976, under the new management of Don Arden, Black Sabbath was able to sort out most of its legal and financial troubles. Arden also found the band a new record producer—NEMS Records in Britain—which was not affiliated with the band's former manager. Arden then sent them on an American tour to promote a compilation album, *We Sold Our Souls for Rock'n'Roll.*

Despite these positive changes, Osbourne became increasingly unhappy working with the band. While he had enjoyed their first few years together, Osbourne had started thinking seriously about quitting the band in the mid-1970s. The legal and business hassles, the personality conflicts, and the grinding routine of touring were alleviated only by the actual performances and by drugs and alcohol. Even making music seemed more and more like work for him. Osbourne later explained his need to separate from the band:

Although Osbourne enjoyed performing, a grueling touring schedule, drug and alcohol abuse, and problems with fellow band members prompted him to consider leaving Black Sabbath in the mid-1970s.

Sabbath falling apart was a natural thing. The fun had gone, like a marriage, y'know. You look at your wife one day and suddenly think, "I don't love you anymore." The best years with Sabbath were up to *Sabbath, Bloody Sabbath* [in 1973], and after that we started to deteriorate. We were . . . on drugs and alcohol, in a terrible state with cocaine and booze and . . . uppers and downers and this and that and pot, and whatever, and we just forgot how to do it together.[24]

In early 1978, after a fight with Tony Iommi, Osbourne quit the band. It is unclear whether he was asked to leave or whether he did it on his own, but he flew back to England and began thinking about starting up his own band. He also went home to be near his father who was terminally ill with bowel cancer. The doctors operated on John Osbourne but were unable to save him. On January 20, 1978, Osbourne's father died.

His father's death greatly upset Osbourne. He had loved his father and watching him die slowly had been very difficult. "What freaked me out more than anything else was the funeral,"[25] he said later. He attended the service, drunk and drugged on Seconal, a depressant, and sang one of Black Sabbath's most popular songs, "Paranoid," to the church.

While the loss of Osbourne's father was hard on him, he took some solace in the fact that his father had lived long enough to see his son become famous. He later recalled: "I was heartbroken when my father died, but at least he saw that I had made something of a success of my life. That meant a lot to me."[26]

Hitting Bottom

After his father's death, Osbourne decided that he had made a mistake by leaving Black Sabbath. He returned to the band only three months after quitting. However, in his absence, Black Sabbath had replaced Osbourne with a new lead singer and songwriter named Dave Walker, formerly of the band Fleetwood Mac. While Osbourne was taken back into the band and Walker was let go, Osbourne was soon unhappy again. He refused to play any of the songs written by Walker and Iommi and became increasingly unreliable. Osbourne stayed in his hotel room away from the others, doing drugs and drinking. He also missed practice often, sometimes for weeks at a time.

The other band members, particularly Iommi, who had stopped drinking and using drugs, were critical of Osbourne's debauchery. Osbourne's excesses were greater than any one else's and it made him unreliable and erratic in his behavior. Although the band produced another album, their ninth album, *Never Say Die!* (1978), the disputes within the band grew to the point where the members barely functioned together. They were less and less interested in working with each other. Finally, when Iommi and Ward met to begin writing songs for a new album, they decided to fire Osbourne. Iommi asked Osbourne to leave the band. According to Osbourne: "Tony [Iommi] didn't want me in the band anymore. I knew what was coming down anyway. . . . I just thought, 'it's over.'" [27]

Osbourne felt that his life had reached a new low after being fired from Black Sabbath. Although he had been unhappy with how things were going with the band, being fired was a blow. In response, he checked into a room at Le Parc Hotel in Los Angeles and spent the next six months there without leaving the room, sending people out for food, alcohol, and drugs. As he remembered: "I wasn't just depressed. I was suicidal. I stayed in a hotel room in Hollywood for . . . months and never opened the drapes. I lived like a slob." [28]

Fortunately for Osbourne, Don Arden had not given up on him. Arden saw that Osbourne was the main talent of Black Sabbath and anticipated that he would be a successful solo performer. When Osbourne was fired, Arden dropped Black Sabbath and decided to offer to represent Osbourne's solo career. He also wanted Osbourne to sign a contract with his record label, Jet.

Arden sent his daughter Sharon to deliver the offer to Osbourne. The simple errand unexpectedly became one of the most important events in Osbourne's and Sharon Arden's lives.

Enter Sharon

Born October 9, 1952, Sharon Arden was born into a show business family. Her father Don Arden had started his career as a singer, and Sharon's mother Noel had been a dancer. After he be-

Ozzy Washed Up?

After being fired from Black Sabbath, Osbourne checked into Le Parc Hotel in Los Angeles and binged on drugs and alcohol to try to forget his troubles. In her biography *Ozzy Unauthorized*, Sue Crawford wrote that Osbourne worried that his career was over.

[Ozzy] would just idle his time away, sitting gazing at the four walls, never leaving his room, never speaking to anyone. To make matters worse, a young music fan lived directly across the road from Ozzy's hotel and every night when he came home from work, he would throw open his windows and blast out Black Sabbath records for hours on end. It was ironic. Ozzy was drinking as hard as he could to forget, but however hard he tried there was always going to be a reminder somewhere. "I was so f—ing lonely. I thought it was the end of me. . . . I just sat around, getting severely loaded and I thought, 'oh well, I'll be out on the streets selling hot dogs in two years, you know? Ozzy Osbourne? Who's he?'"

came a show business manager, Don regularly brought home famous entertainers. Some of Sharon's earliest childhood memories involved meetings with entertainers such as Bill Haley (of Bill Haley and His Comets) and Little Richard. In that environment, Sharon was naturally drawn toward show business, and at fifteen she quit school to work for her father to learn his business.

Sharon Arden first met Ozzy Osbourne when she was eighteen years old. She was working in her father's office as a receptionist when Black Sabbath came in for one of their first meetings with Don. At the time, Sharon was a quiet and timid girl. She remembered being alarmed and frightened by Ozzy, who had arrived for the meeting in his usual outlandish attire. According to Sharon: "Ozzy walked into my father's office without shoes, with a water faucet dangling from his neck and sat on the floor. I was terrified."[29] Sharon Arden was so afraid of Ozzy that when he asked her for a cup of tea, she made one of the other office staff members deliver the cup to him.

However, Sharon did not remain a timid young woman for long. After working as a receptionist, she learned how to represent her father's clients. Modeling herself after her father, she worked hard to learn the business and became a shrewd and tough-minded business manager. She traveled on the road with

Sharon Arden's Musical Childhood

Raised by former singer-turned-music promoter Don Arden and dancer Hope Arden, Sharon Arden developed a love of music early on. In an October 2002 interview with journalist Chris Heath for a *Rolling Stone* magazine article entitled "The Most Loved and Feared Woman in the Music Business on How She Got to Be That Way," Sharon Arden (Osbourne) talked about some of her early memories.

> My father and mother were in the music industry, my mother's mother was in the music industry, and I was, like third genera-tion, and it was like you don't do anything else. There is nothing else. . . . Putting Bill Haley on a train to Europe at Victoria sta-tion in London. 'Cause my dad had him over from America to do a European tour. And then after that, it was Sam Cooke. I fell madly in love with Sam Cooke at age seven. He used to wear these high-cut matador trousers, and he was built a little bit like Prince, so he had a really neat little body. His cologne was so gorgeous that I could smell where he'd been backstage, and I can remem-ber cowering when he'd come out. I mean, how lucky am I? I was weaned on Little Richard, Jerry Lee Lewis, the Everly Brothers, Brenda Lee, Gene Vincent.

bands her father represented, including a few weeks with Black Sabbath in the late 1970s. Sharon became so good at her job that Don sometimes allowed her to act as his representative. Such was the case when he sent her to Ozzy's hotel room to offer to repre-sent the singer's solo career.

Rescuing Ozzy

Since their first meeting, Sharon Arden had become tougher and more savvy about dealing with performers, so she was no longer intimidated by Ozzy Osbourne. She knew Osbourne by his rep-utation, and she considered him a lazy drunk who had thrown his career away. However, when she arrived, she was not prepared for what she found. His room was filthy and unkempt, filled with empty pizza boxes, empty liquor bottles, and drug paraphernalia. Osbourne was depressed, drunk, and stoned. She later remembered: "He was like a squashed man. . . . Stuck in a hotel room with no band, and he just wants to sit there taking drugs. He was just not helping himself." [30]

Unexpectedly, she felt great sympathy for him She decided that she wanted to help him, but decided that she could not cod-

dle him. He needed to be shaken up. Osbourne recalled that
Arden took charge of his life. "She said to me, you clean your
act up."[31]

Years later, Arden recalled that she chose to help Osbourne
because she liked him, in spite of her first impression of him

*Sharon Arden helped Osbourne to get back on his feet after he was fired
from Black Sabbath, and she encouraged him to launch a solo career.*

years earlier. Later, she remembered what attracted her to
Osbourne:

> I thought, "Oh my God, this guy is so vulnerable. He's a
> teddy bear." He wasn't one of those rockers that wanted
> to act the big star. I'd been used to these people going,
> "Bring me, fetch me, wipe my arse." But he wasn't like that
> at all. Also . . . he was gorgeous-looking. He had the best
> smile." [32]

By the close of the 1970s, Osbourne's professional and personal lives were disasters. After a year without work and months
of constant substance abuse, Osbourne was broke, strung out, and
suicidal. However, Arden saw that Osbourne was wasting his
talent on self-pity, drugs, and alcohol. She was convinced that she
was the woman who could do something to change his direction
and make him a success once again.

Chapter 3

Ozzy and Sharon: Starting Over

Ozzy Osbourne and Sharon Arden teamed up for the first time as talent and manager in 1980, and doing so dramatically changed both of their lives. During the early 1980s, Arden and Osbourne together successfully relaunched Osbourne's career. As their professional relationship grew, so too did their personal relationship. However, they also faced several difficult challenges, tragedies, and controversies.

Starting Over

After being out of work for a year, Osbourne was broke by the time Arden rescued him from his six-month drug and alcohol binge. When Thelma Osbourne had kicked him out of their home in England, he had walked away from all of his belongings. He also had spent the severance money he had received when he left Black Sabbath. Arden and Osbourne knew only one way to make money: music. As his new manager, Arden insisted that Osbourne get back to work immediately. She arranged for Osbourne to audition musicians to start a new band. With Arden keeping Osbourne focused and motivated, within a few days he hired three musicians to fill out the band, including guitarist Randy Rhoads, bassist Bob Daisley, and drummer Lee Kerslake. The four-man band recorded their first album, *Blizzard of Ozz,* in mid-1980.

Although Don Arden's company Jet Records was ready to release the album in the UK, Sharon Arden and Osbourne wanted to find an American producer for the new album other than

Sharon's Management Techniques

Like her father, Don Arden, Sharon Osbourne developed a reputation as a savvy and tough show-business manager. In an October 2002 interview with journalist Chris Heath for a *Rolling Stone* magazine article entitled "The Most Loved and Feared Woman in the Music Business on How She Got to Be That Way," she discussed some of her unconventional and often violent tactics for defending her clients' business interests.

> John Scher . . . [was] a very big promoter—or was—in New York, and I was just a twenty-six-year-old kid going in to collect payment for the show that Ozzy had done. It had sold out the first day. So I went in, and he'd got all these bills for advertising up until the week of the show, and I'm like, "You couldn't have advertised, because we sold out the first week." And he said, "Oh, well, it was pre-booked and we had to pay it."—the usual. . . . And he would not give in, and he was threatening that "Ozzy will never work in the New York area again." . . . So I got up and nutted him [hit him in the head] with my head, and then I kicked him in the balls. He just stood there. He was just so taken aback. . . . I never, ever worked with him again, and he never worked with me. And he is now, I think, out of the business. Or he should be.

Warners, since Warners was still Black Sabbath's American distribution company.

Arden made a deal with CBS Records in New York to pay Osbourne sixty-five thousand dollars to produce *Blizzard of Ozz* in the United States. Arden and Osbourne flew to the CBS Records offices in January 1980 for their first in-person meeting with the marketing executives.

Arden wanted Osbourne to make a strong impression on the executives, so she planned a stunt in which Osbourne would carry three doves with him in the sleeves of his jacket and release them during the meeting as a surprise. Things did not go as planned, however. Osbourne showed up to the meeting drunk, and when he released the doves, one of them fell, dead, on the conference table in front of him. Deciding that he could give the executives something to remember, Osbourne picked up the bird and bit off its head. Arden thought it was hilarious.

Others did not find the act humorous. The CBS Records executives were alarmed at the stunt and banned Osbourne from returning to the building (even though they still agreed to be his

American producer). Newspaper and magazine stories reported the incident, casting Osbourne as a madman, and the American Humane Society spoke out against him, calling for a ban of Osbourne's concerts throughout the United States.

Ozzy's Back

Despite the controversy, when *Blizzard of Ozz* was released in September 1980 in the UK (and March 1981 in the United States),

Osbourne grins with blood on his face after biting the head off of a dead dove at his meeting with CBS Records.

it sold very well. It reached no. 7 and no. 21 on the UK and U.S. charts, respectively, and quickly sold more than 4 million copies.

The next step in Arden's plan to revive Osbourne's career was to have his band perform an international tour. Arden set up the tour, with the first performance in Glasgow, Scotland, on September 12, 1980. Osbourne was uneasy about performing his first concert after Black Sabbath. Afraid that he had lost his audience, he paced the streets of Glasgow before the show. Because in Glasgow concert tickets were not sold before the day of the concert, there was no way of knowing how many people would show up until Osbourne walked out on stage that night. His fears proved unfounded, however. The crowd was large and responsive to Osbourne. He was so happy that he could make it without Black Sabbath, that he wept with relief while onstage.

Madman?

In 1981, Osbourne and his band recorded their second album, *Diary of a Madman,* which was released in October of that year. Although the album did not do quite as well commercially—only going to no. 14 on the UK charts and no. 16 in the United States—critics said that the album confirmed that Osbourne's solo career was more than just a one-album phenomenon.

The band again went on tour for the album. The Diary of a Madman tour reinforced Osbourne's reputation as a wild performer. The performances included Ozzy dressing up as an executioner and pretending to execute a dwarf as part of the finale. Arden and Osbourne also arranged for a large catapult to be installed onstage, which he used to hurl pieces of raw meat and offal (animal parts) at the audience at the end of each show. Soon, audiences responded by throwing meat back. Some brought dead animals to throw on stage. False rumors circulated that at one performance Osbourne threw three small dogs into an audience and refused to play until they were all sent back to him dead. At one show, when an audience member threw a baby doll on stage wrapped in a blanket, Osbourne was horrified, thinking at first that it was a real baby.

The Diary of a Madman tour was plagued by mishaps and misfortune. Osbourne's band was turned away from performing

Osbourne holds up a plaque honoring the commercial success of Blizzard of Ozz *and* Diary of a Madman, *Ozzy's first two solo albums.*

in one town because of his reputation. Equipment failures repeatedly occurred, and in Minneapolis, Minnesota, a crane used to set up the stage fell and destroyed thousands of dollars worth of equipment. Then, on January 20, 1982, when the band performed in Des Moines, Iowa, one of the most infamous events of Osbourne's career occurred. At this performance, as had become customary, fans threw raw and rotting meat and dead animals onstage. One fan threw a live bat on stage during the concert. Osbourne thought it was a toy and bit its head off only to discover that it was real. The audience responded by cheering, but Osbourne remembers the shock of realizing it was real:

> Sharon told me later that she saw its wings flapping from the side of the stage, but I didn't. I just picked it up and put it in my mouth in the excitement of the show. I mean

. . . biting a bat's bloody [head] off! It's not very nice to taste—a fresh bat's head—it's all crunchy and warm.[33]

Osbourne had to be taken to the hospital after the concert for a series of rabies vaccinations. A good sport, Osbourne started barking like a rabid dog at the nurses. However, others did not think the event was funny. Osbourne's critics took advantage of the event, using it as proof that he was a madman and a menace. One letter to the editor of an Omaha, Nebraska, newspaper was typical of the sentiment against Osbourne:

> Ozzy Osbourne should be banned for the sake of the community's mental health. . . . This music and what it represents is truly evil. Nothing good can come of it. The writing is on the wall. The negative aspects of this type of music are already apparent.[34]

Although he was used to negative publicity, Osbourne and Arden were amused by the amount and force of the criticism. She later said,

Osbourne was amused by the critics' response to his onstage antics. Here, Ozzy pokes fun at his reputation as a madman by pretending to bite off a dove's head.

It's something that was a complete and utter mistake. And then . . . it's on the morning news and we're laughing. And we're like, "Why would they put this on the news? It's so stupid." [35]

Nonetheless, the bat-biting incident became a well-publicized controversy as animal rights groups again criticized Osbourne. The incident became infamous, which led to rumors that Osbourne drank blood and performed animal sacrifices. It also became a joke for talk-show hosts and newspaper and magazine writers, and became a permanent part of the lore about Osbourne and his career.

Alamo

Just a month after the Des Moines concert, Osbourne provided his critics with more ammunition to use against him when he was arrested in San Antonio while on tour in Texas. Osbourne had been drinking excessively at his hotel one night and Arden put him to bed in his room. She took all of his clothing away, hoping this would keep him in his room and out of trouble. However, when Osbourne woke the next morning with a desire to sightsee, he did not let the lack of clothing stop him. He put on one of Arden's dresses and went out. He began drinking early and became intoxicated. Soon, he had to go to the bathroom. Instead of seeking out a toilet, he urinated against the nearest building, only to be interrupted by a police officer, who arrested him. As it turned out, the building was the Alamo, a historical monument to the 180 people who died fighting against the Mexican army at the site in 1836.

Osbourne was charged with desecration of a national shrine. When he was released, he was fined and banned from performing in San Antonio. The ban remained in effect until 1992, when Osbourne apologized and made a ten-thousand-dollar donation to the caretakers of the Texas shrine.

Osbourne later attributed the incident to his alcoholism and drug use: "I can honestly say that all the bad things that ever happened to me were directly attributed to drugs and alcohol. I mean, I would never urinate at the Alamo at nine o'clock in the morning dressed in a woman's evening dress sober." [36]

Losing Friends

Even Osbourne's highly publicized exploits in Des Moines and San Antonio were insignificant setbacks compared to what happened the next month. Continuing the Diary of a Madman tour, Osbourne and his band traveled to Leesburg, Florida, for a concert. There, Osbourne lost his best friend and lead guitarist Randy Rhoads, as well as two of the band's crew members, to a freak accident. The band was to perform at a mansion in Leesburg on the evening of March 19, and Osbourne and several others slept through the morning in the tour bus outside the mansion to rest up before the show.

Andrew Aycock, the band's bus driver and an amateur pilot, borrowed a small plane from the grounds to give a few members of the band and crew a ride to pass time. On his second trip up, Aycock took Rhoads and the band's makeup artist and hairdresser, Rachel Youngblood. On that flight, Aycock flew close, or "buzzed," the tour bus twice, then on the third time came too close. One of the wings clipped the bus and the plane crashed into the mansion, killing everyone on board. After the collision, the mansion caught fire, and Arden ran into the bus and woke Osbourne, who went outside to see what was happening. According to Arden and Osbourne, Osbourne then ran into the mansion to save a deaf man who had gotten trapped by the fire because he did not hear the accident.

Osbourne was very distraught over losing his friends, particularly Rhoads, with whom he had become very close. He said of Rhoads: "I loved him as a person. . . . I suppose at that time when he died, a part of me died with him because he was the first person who came into my life and gave me hope." [37]

Arden and Osbourne canceled a few shows, and they attended Rhoads's funeral where Osbourne served as a pallbearer. In his depression over the accident, Osbourne began drinking even more heavily than usual. Arden understood his feeling: "You lose your best friend and it's like you can never replace it. You can't forget it. It's something that will always haunt, I know, me and Ozzy for the rest of our lives." [38] However, she made sure that Osbourne did not succumb to the depression that he had experienced after being fired from Black Sabbath. She insisted that he get back to

Osbourne poses with his lead guitarist Randy Rhoads (right). Rhoads's death in March 1982 devastated Ozzy.

work and audition a new guitarist to finish out the tour. Osbourne listened to Arden and hired a replacement. He recalled his emotional state at the time:

> In the few short years before Randy died, I had gone through so much. My father had died, I got kicked out of Sabbath—I was up and down, up and down. Then Randy got killed. At that point I said to Sharon "I can't keep doing this," and she said, "Yes you can. If Randy was alive,

this is what he'd want you to do." So I decided the best thing to do was to get back out on the road. And it wasn't the most amazing show, but we did it.[39]

Hello to Romance

Through the successes and troubles of Osbourne's first two years as a solo performer, he relied heavily on Arden. She was a smart and effective businesswoman and was not afraid to stand up to him. From the start, Arden and Osbourne were attracted to each other, and within months of working together, the two started a romance. Arden recalled that spending so much time together helped their relationship develop: "We were working together every day. We bonded. And one thing led to another. We were in each other's lives 24 hours a day and that's how we fell in love."[40]

By the time Osbourne's divorce from his first wife, Thelma Osbourne, was finalized in January 1981, he and Arden were living and working together as a couple. Many people thought that Osbourne and Arden's romantic relationship would not work out. They were both hot-tempered people who frequently became violent with each other. Arden said, "Our fights were legendary. . . . At a gig, Ozzy would run off-stage during a guitar solo to fight with me, then run back on to finish the song."[41] Like Osbourne, Arden struggled with excessive drinking and was addicted to tranquilizers. She said: "I was a Quaalude freak. That was my excuse for f—ing up everything."[42]

Marriage and Mayhem

The combination of their personalities did not seem to make for a promising marriage, and many of their friends and associates told them so when they became engaged. Arden remembers that she and Osbourne had to get engaged several times because they repeatedly fought and broke off the engagement: "We had five different engagement rings. Every time Ozzy would ask me to marry him, we'd have an argument and I'd throw the damn thing out the window." She accepted only after "we'd spent two days combing through the gardens of a hotel for a $10,000 diamond."[43]

After the long and tragic Diary of a Madman tour, Osbourne and Arden and their friends flew to the island of Maui for their wedding. The couple was married on July 4, 1982, a date chosen so that Osbourne would be able to easily remember it. At the wedding reception, Osbourne did not like the traditional Hawaiian band that was playing, so he kicked them out and he and his band played acoustic versions of some old Black Sabbath and Beatles songs to the guests.

On Their Own

In addition to becoming partners in marriage, Ozzy and Sharon Osbourne wanted to break off on their own professionally. Sharon had managed Osbourne's solo career without much help from her father, and she wanted to continue doing so without having to pay her father a percentage of their profits.

Don Arden was not supportive of the decision and made the break difficult for his daughter. When the deal was settled, Ozzy and

Sharon Osbourne bought their way out of their management contract with Arden for $3 million and the commitment for Osbourne to record one more album for Jet Records.

The Osbournes agreed, but the deal created a long-standing grudge between Sharon Osbourne and her father, which lasted for almost twenty years. She recalled being disappointed that her father made it so professionally and personally difficult for her and Osbourne to break away:

> When I left my father, I left everything. I had nothing, absolutely nothing. All the jewels had gone, everything. Ozzy was broke because he'd just gone through a divorce and literally walked out the

Ozzy and Sharon Osbourne were married in Maui on July 4, 1982.

door and left everything. . . . I didn't have a plan, I didn't
have anything. I just went in feet first and bulldozed my way
into it. And it was very difficult because people were still very
intimidated by my father, and our parting was not amicable.
It was very, very bad. So people were scared to talk to me
because of my father.[44]

To free themselves professionally from Arden, Osbourne
quickly recorded the album for Jet. Released in November 1982,
it was called *Talk of the Devil*, and comprised mostly Black Sabbath
covers recorded live at the Ritz Club in New York. Despite the
quick effort, *Talk of the Devil* was a successful album, charting at
no. 21 in the UK and no. 14 in the United States.

One last final condition in Arden's release of Osbourne was
that his daughter send Osbourne to the Betty Ford Clinic to clean
up his drug and alcohol addictions. Osbourne checked in, but
when he found out that the clinic did not have a bar, he left. He
had assumed that the clinic would teach him to drink without getting sick.

Feuding with Father

When Sharon Osbourne broke away from her father to manage Ozzy
Osbourne on her own, it began a feud with Don Arden that lasted almost twenty years. While she admitted that she was definitely her father's daughter because she was a tough manager like him, there was
a lot about him that Sharon Osbourne did not want to emulate. In the
1980s, Don Arden, who calls himself the "Al Capone of rock," faced trial
for false imprisonment and blackmail of business associates. Although
he was acquitted, his son David Arden was found guilty of the same
charge and was jailed. In a May 2001 interview with journalist Ian Gittins
for London's *Guardian* newspaper, Sharon Osbourne said: "The best les-
son I ever had was watching him [mess] his business up. He taught
me everything not to do. My father's never even seen any of my three
kids, and as far as I'm concerned he never will."

After almost two decades of silence between father and daughter, Don
Arden reentered Sharon Osbourne's life when news came that he was going to publish a biography of his daughter and would tell intimate details of her youth. Although this only further aggravated her, she and
her father made amends on September 11, 2001, after terrorists attacked
the World Trade Center while Ozzy and Sharon Osbourne were staying in
New York on business. The planned biography has not been published.

Bark at the Moon

Free from Arden's management, Ozzy and Sharon Osbourne went to work setting up and recording Osbourne's first solo album produced without Jet Records. Released in December 1983 by CBS Associates, the album, called *Bark at the Moon,* was given rave reviews by critics and charted at no. 24 and no. 19 in the UK and United States, respectively. Osbourne's companion video for the title track "Bark at the Moon" was released with the album, featuring Osbourne dressed as a werewolf, wearing an elaborate costume and makeup, which took eight hours to put on.

However, the success of the album was tempered by tragedy. The same month of its release, a twenty-year-old Canadian man from Halifax, named James Jollimore, committed murder after listening to the album. Jollimore claimed that he had felt so strange while listening to the song "Bark at the Moon" that he went out afterward and stabbed to death a forty-four-year old woman and her two sons. Critics of Osbourne claimed that his music was to blame for the deaths.

Ozzy Back on Top

While the controversies over his music and behavior drew criticism, Osbourne was still extremely popular among his fans. In fact, it seemed that the wilder and more outrageous his exploits and the more negative attention he received in the media, the more his fans loved him. Each of his solo albums sold millions of copies and each charted well in Great Britain and America. On tour, he played to huge, sold-out concert venues all over the world. One concert in San Bernardino, California, in 1983 sold out 350,000 tickets.

By the mid-1980s, Osbourne was back on top of his career. However, many of Ozzy and Sharon Osbourne's greatest accomplishments and challenges were still ahead.

Chapter 4

Ozzy and Sharon: Working Through It

FROM THE MID-1980s to the early part of the new millennium, Ozzy and Sharon Osbourne experienced several dramatic professional and personal successes and setbacks. With the rebirth of Osbourne's career under Sharon's management, the couple became multimillionaires. However, during these years, Osbourne and his music came under attack in the media and in court.

The Osbournes' personal life also fluctuated between highs and lows, as they embarked on a new life together as a family. While Ozzy and Sharon Osbourne were thrilled to become parents, his alcoholism and drug abuse continued to do damage to his and Sharon's relationship and their family, in spite of his several attempts to beat his addictions. However, through their professional and personal ups and downs, Ozzy and Sharon Osbourne persistently fought and worked through their troubles to keep their marriage alive.

New Family

Ozzy and Sharon Osbourne decided to start a family soon after they married. Sharon became pregnant almost immediately, but she miscarried three times before successfully giving birth to their first child in 1983. On September 2, their first daughter, Aimee Rachel was born. The following year daughter Kelly Lee was born on October 27, and their son Jack was born on November 8, 1985.

While Osbourne tried hard to keep in touch with his three children by his first marriage, he had not seen much of them since Thelma Osbourne threw him out for, among other things, his alcohol and drug abuse. Now that he was a father again, Osbourne admitted that his addictions were a problem. The day after Kelly's birth in 1984, Osbourne decided to try to stop his drinking and drug use and checked himself into the Betty Ford Clinic for the second time to try to sober up. He said:

> I was sick and tired of being sick and tired. . . . If it wasn't a sniff of cocaine, it was a pill. If it wasn't a pill it was a smoke of dope. If it wasn't dope, it was a bottle of booze.[45]

While his first session at Betty Ford had not been at all successful, after being released in 1984, Osbourne felt good and stayed sober for a few months. That year, for the first time in more than a decade, Osbourne celebrated New Year's Eve sober, drinking soda instead of alcohol.

Ozzy and Sharon pose with their daughters, Aimee (right) and Kelly. After Kelly's birth, Osbourne decided to quit drinking and using drugs.

Suicide Solution

However, just as his personal life was improving, Osbourne became the defendant in two almost identical lawsuits that brought him a great deal of negative publicity. On October 27, 1984, a nineteen-year-old Osbourne fan, John McCollum, shot himself in the head with a pistol after listening to Osbourne's song "Suicide Solution" from his *Blizzard of Ozz* album. The coroner in the case concluded that McCollum committed suicide "while listening to devil music."[46] His parents brought a lawsuit against Osbourne and CBS Records, the album's producer. Then, in May 1986, sixteen-year-old Michael J. Waller, the son of a Georgia minister, also killed himself after listening to "Suicide Solution." In April 1988, Waller's father filed a wrongful death lawsuit against Osbourne, CBS Records, and several other parties.

Mr. Waller accused Osbourne and other musicians of cynically influencing their fans to do harm to themselves:

> They [musicians] know what they are putting out. There are people who are out there trying to make money, and they have no hesitation to sell your kids down the drain. You see a perfectly normal kid there who doesn't show any signs of depression at all. Then six hours later, he's dead. Nobody can explain it. The only thing we know is that he was listening to this music.[47]

The plaintiffs also alleged that the song contained subliminal messages buried in the recording of the song which caused their son to shoot himself.

Defending the Music

This sort of criticism was not new to Osbourne. Parents, religious groups, and others had frequently blamed Osbourne for his music's influence (and that of his former band mates from Black Sabbath) for such tragedies; however, some defenders of free speech pointed out that there was no cause and effect relationship between his music and such tragedies. In her book *Diary of a Madman*, critic Carol Clerk writes:

> This is a cross that Ozzy has had to bear throughout his career. While distraught parents have accused him of en-

couraging their children to kill themselves or others, Ozzy has rather acted as a magnet for the sort of teenagers who were already likely to commit such acts. [48]

In response to the charges, Osbourne defended his First Amendment right to freedom of speech. He also said that the song was, in fact, about the dangers of alcohol, inspired by the death of former AC/DC musician Bon Scott, who had died one winter night from hypothermia after passing out in his car drunk. According to Osbourne:

> The actual song is a warning about the danger of alcohol and drinking yourself to death. [The lyrics are] "Wine is fine, but whisky's quicker; suicide is slow with liquor. . . ." It wasn't my intention to say, go crazy, kill yourself. It's not a smart career move [to tell your fans to kill themselves], is it? [49]

Osbourne's attorney in the *Waller v. Osbourne, et al.* case, David M. Bass, said that the court cases against Osbourne were important because if Osbourne lost such a case over a fan's misunderstanding of a song's lyrics, it would severely damage the First Amendment protection artists have for their work. "If Ozzy were to lose this type of a case, anyone who misconstrued the lyrics of a song could go out and sue the artist and recover some huge sum of money because they had some bizarre interpretation or bizarre emotional reaction to music and that would be the end of what we understood to be freedom of speech." [50]

Osbourne's song "Suicide Solution" was inspired by the alcohol-related death of Bon Scott of the band AC/DC.

"Pornography in Sound"

Ozzy Osbourne was a controversial performer from the beginning of his career; later on, during the early 1990s, he and his music served as a point of attack for many conservative religious and political leaders who pressed for music censorship. For example, in 1990, Osbourne's music—particularly his song "Suicide Solution"—was publicly attacked by conservative Cardinal John O'Connor in a speech given at St. Patrick's Cathedral in New York. In the speech, O'Connor accused heavy-metal music of leading people to suicide and drugs. Quoted by journalist Jim Pfiffer in the March 6, 1990, issue of *USA Today*, he singled out Osbourne's "Suicide Solution" as guilty of harm, calling the song "pornography in sound."

Osbourne was upset by O'Connor's remarks and responded with a public statement, quoted in the March 7, 1990, issue of the *St. Louis Post-Dispatch*. It read: "You are ignorant about the true meaning of my songs. . . . I am offended and deeply hurt by your remarks about me. If you want to discuss this matter with me personally, you can call me any time and I will only be too happy to discuss this with you in private. God bless you."

Many in the press wrote in defense of Osbourne. For instance, in the March 17, 1990, issue of the *St. Louis Post-Dispatch*, journalist Taylor Kingston wrote an editorial attacking O'Connor's logic. It read:

Cardinal John O'Connor has only damaged his credibility by his recent remarks linking rock music and Satanism. The alleged Satanic trappings of certain heavy-metal bands are merely showbiz gimmicks, and their supposed influence exists far more in the fevered imaginations of fanatics than in fact. Rock music no more causes demonic possession than a Dracula movie turns one into a vampire. O'Connor's citing of Ozzy Osbourne as an ally of the devil is ludicrous.

Cardinal John O'Connor denounced Osbourne's music as Satanic and harmful.

The plaintiffs argued that the First Amendment protection regarding freedom of speech did not apply because speech that excites people to do illegal or harmful things is not protected. Nonetheless, both lawsuits were decided in Osbourne's favor. In the *Waller v. Osbourne, et al.* case, presiding Judge Duross Fitzpatrick ruled that the lyrics of "Suicide Solution" discussed the phenomenon in a "philosophical" sense, rather than personally recommending to Waller that he take his own life; therefore, Osbourne and the other defendants had not engaged in "culpable excitement," which would have superseded the First Amendment right to freedom of speech.

Ozzy, Ozzy Everywhere

Despite the negative publicity Osbourne received due to the lawsuits, the late 1980s were a productive time for his career. He released three popular albums: *The Ultimate Sin* (1986), a tribute album to Randy Rhoads called *Tribute* (1987), and *No Rest for the Wicked* (1988). Each album made the charts in Britain and the United States and sold millions of copies.

Additionally, Osbourne's video compilation of his Ultimate Sin tour was released in 1986 and sold more than five hundred thousand copies. Then in 1987, Osbourne appeared in his first feature film, *Trick or Treat,* playing the part of a minister. Osbourne enjoyed playing the part after having been falsely portrayed in the press as a Satanist. He also generally enjoyed being on film and continued to appear in films and videos, often as himself in cameo appearances.

Finally, Sharon Osbourne arranged for Osbourne to appear in his first pay-per-view concert on cable television, in which viewers could receive the live broadcast of his performance for a fee. The performance was held at Tower Theater in Philadelphia, and the audience was one of the largest pay-per-view audiences to date at the time.

Battling Alcohol

Although Osbourne's professional success was making himself and his family increasingly wealthy and famous, his personal life was again becoming strained because of his alcoholism and drug use. He struggled to control his habits in an effort to be a good influence on his young children, remembering that he had lost his first family because of his excesses. He continually vowed to clean up but would end up turning to alcohol and drugs when he was depressed or when he was on tour. His visits to drug rehabilitation centers increased. Years later, he looked back on his addiction and how drugs and particularly drinking were turning him into a split personality: "It's a total Dr. Jekyll and Mr. Hyde experience.... No one is the same person under the influence of alcohol as they are sober.... You take [alcohol] to change. That's the reason for it. But I didn't like the person I was changing into but I couldn't stop."[51]

Sharon Osbourne also remembers his personality changes, saying Osbourne was emotionally and physically abusive while drinking, apologetic when sober. Although she considered leaving Osbourne, she stayed with him to keep the family together. She said:

> There were a lot of times when I was very, very frightened of him. . . . I was a beaten woman. When women are abused and they go back, I know how they feel. You have no self-esteem, no self-respect, you're worthless. . . . In the mornings he'd wake up and be the Ozzy that I love. He'd be sweet and he'd be sorry for his behavior the night before, and loving, and gorgeous. And then by 10 P.M. at night he'd be gone again. It was those few hours of the day that kept me there. Also we had children. And I did not want my children to come from a broken home. I couldn't think of anything worse. I had three babies, a husband that I loved but who was a lunatic. What do you do? You stay and you try to work through it.[52]

The worst incident related to Osbourne's addiction came in September 1989. In August, Osbourne had performed in Russia at the Moscow Music Peace Festival and had received a case of Russian vodka as a gift. On the night of September 2, after celebrating their daughter Aimee's sixth birthday at a Chinese restaurant, Osbourne came home and drank three bottles of the vodka. He became very drunk and tried to strangle Sharon Osbourne, telling her, "We've decided that you've got to go."[53]

Osbourne performs on tour in the late 1980s. Osbourne drank heavily while on tour, and he often abused his wife when he was drunk.

Sharon Osbourne recounted the incident: "[The drink] sent him crazy. He really did go mad. It was terrifying. I mean, me and my old man have had fist fights before, we've broken up rooms and all that, you know, but never anything like this."[54]

Fortunately for Sharon, the Osbournes' house was equipped with an emergency alarm, which Sharon was able to set off. The police arrived in time to save Sharon from being killed. They arrested Osbourne and took him to jail. When he woke up the next morning, Osbourne had no memory of the incident. He said:

> I thought I'd gotten drunk and somebody had dumped me at the police station. Then I go out to court and there's eight million press cameras and I get charged with attempted

murder because I tried to strangle Sharon . . . which is the last thing in my mind. I love the woman. To this day, I still have no clue about that night.[55]

Sharon decided not to press charges against her husband, but instead had him sent into drug and alcohol treatment. She also took out a court order to prevent Osbourne from approaching the house or Sharon and the children while he was in treatment.

Osbourne spent the next three months in rehabilitation, missing his family terribly. One day Sharon received a package at the house from her husband. Inside, she found all of his hair, which he had cut off as a form of apology. He also included a note that said he was sorry.

Turning the Tables

While the incident was hard on the family, Sharon Osbourne looked back on the separation as an important and valuable time

After attempting to strangle Sharon while drunk, Osbourne spent three months in rehabilitation trying to overcome his addictions.

for her to regain some of the self-esteem she felt she had lost over the years of living with Osbourne and his abuse. She said:

> It was the best thing that ever happened. Because during those three months, the tables turned. I regained my strength as a person. I could answer back. It changed our relationship. . . . When he got out, he was very low-key, very timid, very apologetic. Like a child. [56]

When Osbourne was released from his rehabilitation treatment, both he and Sharon knew that he had not completely cleaned up. In 1990, he continued to drink. Osbourne often reverted to drinking out of habit. He said:

> To go into a center like Betty Ford Center and come out a new man—well, they give you the tools in there, but if you slip, you slip. It's like anything. You think, one or two [drinks] won't hurt. But you have one, you have two, you have 10, you start again. [57]

No More Tears, No More Madman

Nineteen ninety-one was a year of great change for the Osbournes, professionally and personally. After several years of going in and out of rehabilitation, Ozzy Osbourne quit drinking and using drugs for a sustained period of time. It was the first time he had been completely sober since he started drinking at the age of fourteen. He was determined not to let his kids grow up around a drunken drug addict, and he sought medical attention to help him stay sober. He was prescribed the antidepressant drug Prozac to help him deal with his emotional troubles—the ones that in the past led him to drink or abuse drugs.

To help maintain his sobriety, Osbourne took up a strenuous exercise regimen that included an hour of stationary bicycling, several hundred sit-ups, and weight training each day. He also changed his diet, eating more vegetables and cutting out red meat. Within months, he lost a lot of weight, toned up his muscles, and felt his mind clear for the first time in decades.

Osbourne said that he was also taking his career in a different direction. After the lawsuits and the accusations of being a

Satanist or madman, he said he was tired of people confusing his stage persona with his real personality: "I'm puttin' Ozzy on the shelf. . . . I'm not going to put out another 'Ozzy Osbourne' album. I created a monster, you know?"[58]

As part of his new musical direction, Ozzy released his ninth solo album, *No More Tears,* which he proudly said was the first album he had ever recorded completely sober and which he had recorded to satisfy himself and nobody else. The album included a mixture of ballads and heavy-metal rock songs. One of the ballads, "Mama I'm Coming Home," was written for Sharon, the title originating from what Ozzy always said to Sharon when he would call home from tour to say he was returning.

Critics responded to the album well, many calling it his finest and most mature album yet. Osbourne joked, saying, "People just say that because I didn't call the album 'Kill Your Mother for Breakfast.'"[59] Nonetheless, the single "I Don't Want to Change the World" from the *No More Tears* album went on to win a Grammy in 1993 for Best Metal Performance.

Don't Blame Me

As part of his effort to change his image, Osbourne agreed to participate in a 1991 documentary, *Ozzy Osbourne: Don't Blame Me.* Directed by Jeb Brien, the film followed the twenty-three years of Osbourne's career to that time, including interviews with both Ozzy and Sharon Osbourne, as well as numerous other musicians associated with Ozzy Osbourne, such as Jon Bon Jovi, Alice Cooper, and Nikki Sixx and Mick Mars of Motley Crue.

Ozzy Osbourne: Don't Blame Me portrayed the story of Osbourne's real life in an effort to dispel misconceptions and rumors about himself and his career. Much of the documentary focused on Osbourne as a family man, including home-movie footage of him and Sharon at their Buckingham home with their three children, who were between six and eight years old at the time.

Growing Up Osbourne

However normal the Osbourne family appeared in their home movies, though, the Osbourne children grew up in an environment that was quite different from that of most children. Since they were

Banned in New Jersey

In 1997, New Jersey concert promoters tried to cancel an Ozzy Osbourne performance because he had signed controversial musician Marilyn Manson to open the concert for him. After several years of assault by critics over his song "Suicide Solution," Osbourne was intolerant of such tactics. He took the promoters to court and won the right for himself and Marilyn Manson to perform. In the June 26, 1997, issue of *Rolling Stone,* journalist John Widerhorn quoted Osbourne's comments on the trial: "On principle we took them to court. . . . If you want to complain about [controversial material such as Marilyn Manson's or "Suicide Solution"], start from the beginning. Start with Shakespeare. What was *Romeo and Juliet* about? Suicide!"

born, Aimee, Kelly, and Jack Osbourne had traveled with their parents all over the world while Ozzy Osbourne toured. In addition to the numerous houses Ozzy and Sharon bought over the years, home for the Osbourne children was the tour buses and the hundreds of hotel rooms the family stayed in.

Being the children of a world-famous rock star was exciting and interesting—the kids travelled, met interesting people, and benefited from their parents' growing wealth. However, as the children grew, it became more difficult for the family to travel together because the children needed to attend school regularly. Osbourne toured alone more frequently, and the long separations from Sharon and the children were hard on him.

Ozzy Retires

In June 1992, Osbourne surprised fans when he and Sharon Osbourne announced that he was retiring from music so that he could spend more time with his children. They announced Osbourne's final tour, called the No More Tours tour, in support of the *No More Tears* album. Although they did not announce it at the time, the Osbournes had additional reasons for Osbourne's retirement plans. After giving up drinking and drugs, Osbourne had developed a serious limp, which Sharon feared was the onset of multiple sclerosis (MS) because of the comments of one doctor. MS is a disease which disrupts the nervous system, causing various symptoms, including limping and difficulty with control of the body. According to biographer Sue Crawford, Sharon

(Left to right) Ward, Iommi, Butler, and Osbourne pose for photographers as Black Sabbath is honored with a star on Hollywood's Rock Walk in November 1992.

Osbourne did not tell her husband of her suspicions about his disease but insisted that he retire. As with most decisions regarding his career, Osbourne simply accepted her wishes.

The No More Tours tour was Osbourne's most successful up to that time. It culminated with a reunion of the original Black Sabbath musicians, Osbourne, Tony Iommi, Geezer Butler, and Bill Ward. They played for what was supposed to be Osbourne's last-ever concert in Costa Mesa, California, on November 15, 1992. Three days later, Black Sabbath was honored with a star on the Rock Walk on Sunset Boulevard in Hollywood. Then in 1993, Osbourne released a double-album recording of the tour.

Retirement Sucks

After the 1992 tour, Sharon took Ozzy to one of America's leading MS specialists to have her suspicions about her husband's condition confirmed. The doctor said that he did not have MS. Sharon was overjoyed, and Ozzy bemused because he never thought he had the disease to begin with.

At first, retirement agreed with Osbourne. He was happy to spend time at home with his wife and three young children, but after awhile he felt the urge to return to work:

I started doing the things I'd always wanted to do. I bought a football and played football with my son. I really enjoyed being a dad . . . for about a week. Then Sharon said to me one day, 'Is that it now? Are you finished?' She let me get all these things out of my system. Then she asked me what I wanted to do. And I said, 'I want to get a band, man.'[60]

Osbourne gathered a new band and went back into the studio to work on his own music again.

Although Ozzy had publicly retired, he wanted to perform and tour again. Sharon understood and helped him market his comeback. In 1995, he released a new album, entitled *Ozzmosis,* and went out on tour, calling it the Retirement Sucks tour. Ozzy and Sharon Osbourne were worried about how the public would respond to Ozzy's return, but their concerns were unnecessary. Ozzy Osbourne was as popular as ever.

Ozzfest

Ozzy was glad to be back on stage and Sharon had the idea to sign up Osbourne with the music festival Lollapalooza. The invention of Perry Farrell, the leader of the band Jane's Addiction, Lollapalooza was a summer rock festival that toured the United States in the mid-1990s. However, when Sharon Osbourne approached the promoters in 1995 to sign up Ozzy to tour with the festival, she was turned down. They did not think that he was a good fit—that he was no longer exciting to the audience of the festival.

Sharon Osbourne was insulted and angry. She decided that if Lollapalooza would not have her husband, then she would create her own festival. In 1996, she put together a festival called Ozzfest with sixteen heavy-metal bands, with Ozzy Osbourne as the top-billed performer. She set up two summer dates, one in Phoenix and the other in Los Angeles. The two dates quickly sold out.

Bob Chiappardi, president of Concert Marketing, remarked that Sharon Osbourne's idea was an excellent move: "Sharon is indeed a very sharp woman. When all the tours were taking off, she realized that there was a need for one that specialized in heavy metal, even if the genre was not popular. Then she branded it with Ozzy's name. . . . Ozzfest has become the keeper of the gate, as far as new metal acts are concerned. If a new band does not make it onto Ozzfest, they know that they are in trouble."[61]

The 1996 Ozzfest was hugely successful, selling out fifty thousand tickets. The following year, Ozzfest became the number one top-grossing per-show summer concert event. Ozzfest continued to grow each year, and by the end of the 1990s it was earning over $20 million in ticket sales. Sharon Osbourne was pleased with the success of the show, realizing that Ozzy Osbourne's draw was what appealed most to the festival audience. She said, "They just love him so much. It makes me so proud. It makes everything worth it."[62]

Ozzy Osbourne attributes the festival's success entirely to his wife. He said: "You know what? [Ozzfest] should really be

Sharon speaks at a news conference about Ozzfest, the popular heavy-metal mucic festival she created.

Osbourne performs at Ozzfest in 1997. The festival's enormous success proved that audiences still loved Ozzy's music.

called Sharon Fest. . . . It's embarrassing for me because she does all the work, the bookings, the deals, and whatever. Sharon is a remarkable woman. And I take her for granted." [63]

Black Is Back

A considerable draw for Ozzfest 2 in 1997 was the reunion of Black Sabbath, which Sharon Osbourne orchestrated. Initially, Bill Ward was the only member of the band absent from the festival; the other members had decided not to ask him because of his ill health, believing he would not be able to tour. Ozzfest 2 played twenty-two shows across America.

Working together again appealed to Osbourne and his former band mates. They decided to perform a reunion concert. Although Ward was suffering ill health from years of heavy drinking and drug use, and had suffered a mild heart attack a few years past, he desperately wanted to be part of the reunion, so he also re-joined the band. The four rehearsed in secret and then gathered in their hometown of Birmingham in December 1997 to perform. The response to the concert was so overwhelmingly positive that they toured the following year as a headliner for Ozzfest. Then, in 1998, they performed a reunion tour separate from Ozzfest and recorded an album together for the first time in twenty years.

The reunion tour, however, was plagued by illnesses, includ-ing the discovery of a noncancerous growth on Osbourne's lar-ynx, which prevented him from performing several concerts. Nonetheless, the concert tour was fun for all of the band mem-bers. They joined up again with Ozzfest 1999 during the summer, and then returned to finish their tour. They called it the Last Supper Tour, as they decided it would be their last tour together. It ended in December 1999, back in Birmingham, where they had started their careers together in 1967. At their final concert, they announced it would be the last time Black Sabbath would ever play together again.

Paying the Price

At the end of 1999, Osbourne was living as clean and sober a lifestyle as he had in over thirty years. He had given up drugs, had his drinking under control, and was working on giving up ciga-rettes. However, his physical and mental health suffered. His doc-tors told him that the years of substance abuse had caused a per-manent chemical imbalance in his brain. The imbalance was in part responsible for some memory loss and a shortened attention span, which made it difficult for Osbourne to concentrate.

Ozzy Osbourne also had developed a stoop and shuffling gait, as well as tremors in his hands, which he and Sharon thought at first was the onset of Parkinson's disease. Fortunately for Osbourne, the tremors turned out to be a non–life threatening, hereditary ail-ment suffered by a number of people in his family.

Osbourne regularly visited a psychiatrist who put him on a regimen of antidepressant drugs. He also continued working out to keep his body in as good a shape as possible. Despite the num-ber of health problems he had, Osbourne felt fortunate that his health had suffered enough to make him stop his addictions. He said: "It's like the old saying, 'You play now, you pay later.' Eventually it'll kick your butt if you're lucky. If you're not lucky, you'll go mad, or you go to jail, or you die."[64]

Osbourne also gave credit to Sharon Osbourne for keeping him from killing himself with his excesses and addictions. He said: "Without my wife, I would be long dead. I just wake up every morning glad I haven't died in my sleep."[65]

Osbourne credits his wife and manager Sharon with saving his life by helping him beat his addictions.

Back on Tour

Despite his health challenges, Ozzy Osbourne continued to work on his music. He headlined Ozzfest each year, and, in 2001, returned to the studios to record his first solo album in six years, called *Down to Earth*. Released on October 16, 2001, by Epic Records in Los Angeles, *Down to Earth* was one of Osbourne's most popular albums, debuting at no. 4 on the American music charts.

In support of the album, Sharon Osbourne arranged a U.S. tour for the album. Called the Merry Mayhem tour, it was Osbourne's first solo tour in six years. The tour commenced on Halloween 2001 in Tucson, Arizona, and was scheduled to travel to several cities in America. However, many of the dates had to be cancelled when Osbourne injured his foot getting out of a hotel shower in November. Unaware of the severity of the injury, Osbourne continued to perform until the pain was so bad that he sought a doctor's opinion. The doctors told him the foot was broken. Osbourne took a few weeks off, resuming the tour at the end of November.

Osbourne played a December 23 concert in Meadowlands, New Jersey, to benefit families of firefighters, police, and other victims of the September 11, 2001, terrorist attack on the World Trade Center. He also visited Ground Zero, where firefighters and police presented him with an iron cross made from steel taken from the wreckage of the World Trade Center buildings.

Sharon Osbourne also arranged an international leg for the Merry Mayhem tour, which included Japan, Korea, Canada, and Germany. As part of the tour, he performed at a USO show for U.S. Army troops stationed in South Korea. He also played a concert at Budokan Hall in Japan, on February 15, 2002, which was recorded and released as an album and video called *Live at Budokan*.

The success of Ozzy Osbourne's career, and the millions of dollars each year in proceeds from Ozzfest, has made the Osbourne family very wealthy. By the spring of 2001, Ozzy, Sharon, and their three children planned to move into a new mansion in Beverly Hills. Sharon Osbourne had negotiated a deal with MTV for the family to appear in ten episodes of an unscripted "reality" program to be filmed in their house from the day they moved in. None of the family was prepared for the effect the program would have on their lives.

Chapter 5

MTV's First Family

In 2001, Ozzy and Sharon Osbourne purchased a new mansion in Beverly Hills and prepared their family to settle in under the watch of MTV camera crews. The experimental reality program captured the details of the Osbournes' everyday life, including family celebrations and squabbles.

No one in the Osbourne family was prepared for how successful the show would become or how much it would affect their lives, particularly the lives of the two youngest Osbourne children, Kelly and Jack Osbourne (the eldest, Aimee Osbourne, chose not to appear in the program). Additionally, the Osbourne family could not have predicted the dramatic ups and downs that their lives would take in the first years of the new century.

The Concept

The idea for a television program based on the daily life of the Osbourne family was inspired in part by the success of two cable network programs on Ozzy Osbourne and his home. In a 2000 episode of the VH1 network's music biography series *Behind the Music,* Osbourne was interviewed about his career. The episode was the series' most popular ever. An Osbourne episode of *Cribs,* an MTV network program in which audiences were given a tour of celebrities' homes, also did very well. Always focused on innovative ways to market her husband's career, Sharon Osbourne began investigating the possibility of doing a show involving the whole family.

Although many networks she spoke to were interested in the concept, they wanted to have the Osbournes appear in scripted shows, like situation comedies. The Osbournes did not want to do that. Sharon recalled: "Everybody that I took it to wanted to kind

Sharon, Kelly, Jack, and Ozzy Osbourne began filming the MTV show documenting their daily lives in October 2001.

of take it and make it their own, sort of like make us a sitcom. And, you know, the typical thing of, you know, they wanted it scripted. They wanted canned laughter. You know, one take after another. And we couldn't do that." [66]

Then, MTV agreed to do an experimental run of ten episodes of unscripted filming. It was agreed that the filming would begin as the Osbourne family moved into their new mansion in Beverly Hills and that the show would focus on the day-to-day life of the family. Although MTV producers were unsure of the experiment, the popularity of the VH1 and MTV episodes in 2000 made it seem like a good risk. The family was paid $575,0000 for ten episodes and the filming of the show began in October 2001.

On Camera

MTV installed film crews in the Osbournes' new house to film the family from the day they moved in until the middle of February 2002. Hidden cameras were used in some rooms, while at other times, camera and sound-recording technicians would follow the family members around, in and outside the house.

At first, the film crew was at the house every day, eighteen hours a day, with the only off-limits areas being Sharon and Ozzy Osbournes' bedroom and the bathrooms. Additionally, the film crew was forbidden in the mansion's guest house in the backyard where the Osbournes' eldest daughter, Aimee Osbourne (who did not wish to participate in the show over concerns of privacy), lived during the filming, and cameras were turned off when she entered the room in the main house. Other than those restrictions, the crew was authorized to capture everything that went on in the house, day or night. However, the family decided that they needed a day free from the crews, so Sundays became their day off from filming.

Although the family eventually adjusted to having the film crews in the house, each family member admitted that there were times they resented the intrusion on their privacy. Ozzy Osbourne said: "Sometimes I forget [about the filming and] as soon as I open the doors, I would be on. I would get kind of quick-tempered, you know, surprised, forgetting they were there. 'Not now, guys,' you know."[67]

The ten episodes of the first season of *The Osbournes* captured the family in their daily routines, in family discussions and arguments, and in celebrations such as Kelly Osbourne's seventeenth birthday and Christmas dinner. The crew filmed hundreds of hours and MTV then edited the footage down, creating thematic episodes based around events in the household. For example, there was an episode called "Won't You Be My Neighbor," which focused on the Osbournes' battling with neighbors over "terrible 'middle-aged' music"[68] coming from the neighbors' house until late at night.

In editing the film for broadcast, the MTV network found that they had to censor, or "bleep," over much of the family's dialogue because of the excessive cussing. Some of the dialogue—particularly Ozzy Osbourne's—became almost unintelligible because nearly every other word was censored.

The Osbournes

The show, called *The Osbournes,* debuted on MTV on March 5, 2002, less than a month after filming stopped. It was an instant hit. During the 2002 viewing schedule, *The Osbournes* became a broadcasting phenomenon. Attracting more than 6 million viewers every week in the United States, it was the highest rated show in MTV's twenty-year history. The program also proved popular in the UK, where it premiered on May 26, 2002, drawing an audience of more than five hundred thousand households. The show finished better than it had started, with the season finale in May 2002 drawing 7.2 million viewers in the United States.

Accolades and Opportunities

In addition to the new recognition and the money, the show created a number of opportunities for the family. Among them was Ozzy and Sharon's invitation from President George W. Bush to attend a press dinner at the White House on May 4, 2002. Ozzy and Sharon Osbourne could not believe that they had been invited, and after the event was over, Sharon Osbourne said, "The whole experience was overwhelming and surreal."[69]

The following month brought another invitation from a world leader. England's Queen Elizabeth was celebrating her Golden Jubilee, the fiftieth anniversary of her reign as monarch on June 3, 2002. Ozzy and Sharon were invited to attend, and Ozzy Osbourne was invited to sing. He was astounded and proud to be asked. He said: "I wish Mum and Dad could have seen it. . . . I can't believe I've been invited to Buckingham Palace."[70]

At the performance, he sang for, and met, the queen. Osbourne was so nervous, he does not recall much about the meeting: "The Queen spoke to me, but I haven't a clue what she said. Look at the photographs. I'm in shock."[71]

The Osbournes also received critical acclaim when the show won an Emmy for Best Reality Program in September 2002. Then, in January 2003, Ozzy, Sharon, Kelly, and Jack Osbourne hosted the thirtieth annual American Music Awards on ABC. True to form, the family gave the censors a lot of work bleeping profane language throughout the broadcast.

Osbourne performs at Queen Elizabeth's Golden Jubilee at Buckingham Palace in June 2002. The concert was part of a celebration honoring the queen's fiftieth anniversary as monarch.

The monetary rewards for the first season of *The Osbournes* put the family on the British Rich List. With a joint fortune of $58 million in 2001, the Osbournes were among the wealthiest in their native country.

Regrets

The show's success profoundly affected the Osbourne family. They were interviewed many times, written about in the media, and became the topic of Internet chat rooms and websites. The immense popularity of the show had turned the family into an international phenomenon. While Ozzy Osbourne and, to some degree, Sharon Osbourne were accustomed to being recognized in public, it was a new experience for Kelly and Jack.

Despite the popularity of the show and the opportunities it provided the family, they had some misgivings about having done it. Sharon Osbourne noted that the unanticipated success had affected her children the most: "Our lives have changed so much. I don't say we're not the same people. But the show has had such an impact on everybody. My kids aren't . . . normal. . . . They have lawyers and business managers."[72]

Indeed, the Osbourne children had unusual childhoods. Growing up splitting their time between England and America, the Osbourne children attended private schools in both countries until high school. Although Ozzy Osbourne was proud that he could afford to send his children to good schools—an opportunity he felt he missed in his own childhood—both Kelly and Jack Osbourne dropped out before finishing high school, like both their parents had done.

While Ozzy Osbourne was disappointed, Sharon Osbourne explained that their children's special circumstance made school socially difficult for them. Their father's infamous reputation as a bat-biting madman set them apart from their classmates, and they were constantly aware of their family's differences from the families of friends and schoolmates, even in Los Angeles and even while attending elite private schools, where they met and socialized with other children of celebrities. Sharon said: "My kids don't fit in. None of them were A-students. . . . Their school is life."[73]

Kelly

The privileges of wealth and celebrity impacted the Osbourne children for most of their lives, but especially since the debut of *The Osbournes.* Kelly Osbourne admitted that growing up rich and famous has been a strong force in her life but that she has tried to remember that others do not have the advantages that she has. She said: "I don't deny that I'm spoiled. I've never needed anything in my life. But if I see a homeless person, I can't walk past them without giving them money."[74]

Although her newfound fame from the television program bothered her at times, she made an effort to understand that part of being a celebrity was to be recognized and approached in public. She said: "It bugs me when people come up and don't go away or touch me. But you know what? I put myself out there so I have to expect people to come up to me and tell me what they think of the show. I would be nothing but nice. It comes with the territory."[75]

Ozzy's Still Got It

In April 2002, Ozzy Osbourne was awarded his own star on Hollywood's Walk of Fame. Osbourne's star is situated next to Marilyn Monroe's. In a July 2002 interview on CTV Television's *Canada AM*, Osbourne marveled at the staying power of his fame. He said: "I remember being in a club and [my] manager at the time said to me, 'Ozzy, I've got some good news. Your album is on the British charts at 17.' And I said, 'You're joking.' . . . And at that point I remember thinking, 'Well this'll do me for another couple of years and that'll be it for me and then I've got to move on.' Here I am, 33 years later, still popular. I mean, it's mind-blowing what's happened to me."

Osbourne poses next to his star on the Hollywood Walk of Fame in April 2002.

Role Model

As one of the unexpected responsibilities of her fame, Kelly Osbourne found herself serving as a role model for young women. Outspoken and honest, Kelly frequently spoke out regarding body image after some newspapers and magazines called her overweight. "People are always horrible about my weight and that's insignificant and stupid. I don't choose to be this weight and I know that if I stopped eating french fries for a week I'd lose some pounds but I like who I am. And I'm not going to sacrifice my happiness just because someone says I'm fat. It doesn't hurt me." [76]

Her refusal to let the comments about her weight interfere with her self-esteem and her potential career won her many fans, particularly among young women her age. As recognition, in December 2002, Kelly Osbourne was named as one of *Rolling Stone* magazine's People of the Year. In an interview with the magazine, she again spoke out against what she saw as the media's unhealthy focus on appearances. "I think people need to start . . . paying less attention to appearance. I'm sorry, but speaking of that, *Rolling Stone* haven't put a fully clothed woman on the cover [of their magazine] in God knows how long." [77]

In addition, clothing designer Lane Bryant invited Kelly Osbourne to sing at their fashion show. Kelly agreed, but was appalled by what was defined as "fat" by the fashion industry. She said: "[Lane Bryant] see me like the signature fat kid, so they want[ed] me to do their show. But most of those women [at the show] were not fat. I think it's disgusting that they were labeled as plus-size. Size 12 is not plus-size." [78]

Kelly's Career

As well as giving her public exposure and making her a role model, the opportunities provided by her newfound celebrity

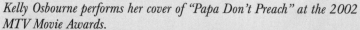

Kelly Osbourne performs her cover of "Papa Don't Preach" at the 2002 MTV Movie Awards.

forced Kelly Osbourne to overcome her indecision about what she wanted to do with her life. She said:

> I had absolutely no idea what I wanted to do with my life. I was actually quite depressed about it. Everyone around me knew what they wanted from life. My sister had this beautiful voice and she was always in the recording studio. My brother was working as a talent scout. I was really upset that I didn't have a clue. I was working in an office, answering the phones. Then the show took off and it blew me away. Suddenly all these opportunities came my way, and I'd have been mad not to take them.[79]

In 2001, Kelly Osbourne got her first recording opportunity when Epic Records—Ozzy Osbourne's record producer—produced *The Osbourne Family Album,* a collection of songs related to the television program. Aimee Osbourne was approached to do a cover of the Madonna song "Papa Don't Preach" for the album. However, she did not want to be involved with the project since it was associated with the show, so she turned it down and suggested her sister Kelly record the song instead.

Although Kelly Osbourne had no musical training, she accepted the opportunity to record the song. The song and an accompanying video were released in July 2002 to surprising success. "Papa Don't Preach" entered the U.S. charts at no. 3 and sold very well. Pleased with the success, Epic executives asked Kelly to do a full-length album.

Shut Up

Kelly collaborated with various songwriters and producer Ric Wake, then went into the studio in late 2002 to record her first album, *Shut Up.* Musically influenced by bands such as the 1970s' Blondie and more recent bands such as Courtney Love's Hole, the album debuted in November 2002. Many critics placed the album among the growing number of punk- and heavy metal–inspired music known as nu metal or nu punk. Critic Leigh Mytton of BBC News Online described the album as a look inside Kelly Osbourne's state of mind: "[Through the album] Kelly is venting her frustrations about boys, authority and feeling misunderstood."[80]

Kelly Osbourne makes a store appearance to promote her album, Shut Up, *in November 2002.*

Despite the success of her single "Papa Don't Preach," Osbourne's *Shut Up* album did not do as well. Critical response to the album was mixed. Few critics liked the entire album, and many gave it decidedly bad reviews. Music critic Maddy Costa of Britain's *Guardian* wrote that while a couple of the songs were good, Osbourne's appeal did not merit a full-length album. She wrote: "Osbourne is a riot in small doses, but you soon wish she would take her own advice and shut up."[81]

By March 2003, the single "Shut Up" had risen to *Billboard* magazine's "Heat Seeker's" chart, a list of songs that had not made the Top 200 but sold well. Kelly Osbourne began a tour of the United States and the UK to promote her album.

In addition to her musical career, since the debut of *The Osbournes,* Kelly Osbourne has also received acting opportunities. Among them was a role in the 2003 remake of Disney's *Freaky Friday* (which she turned down) and a starring role in a series of commercials for Doritos, which launched in March 2003.

Jack

Just as Kelly Osbourne set off on a similar career path as her father, Jack Osbourne also entered show business at an early age;

however, he followed his mother's example, deciding he wanted to work offstage.

During his school years, Jack Osbourne experienced many of the same frustrations that his father had, including learning disabilities, which led him to leave school at the age of sixteen. He said: "I was dyslexic and a real hyper kid. I couldn't focus, so that affected my grades. I dropped out [in 2002]."[82] However, his mother thinks that Jack is very street smart and intelligent. She said: "Jack knows a lot about everything and has a wonderful vocabulary. He's very worldly."[83]

After he dropped out, Jack began working full time with his mother at Epic Records in Los Angeles as a talent scout. He spent much of his time in clubs trying to find promising new bands for Epic to record. He also got his first chance to produce a song when his sister Kelly recorded "Papa Don't Preach" in 2002.

Like the other members of the Osbourne family, Jack works in the music business. He is a talent scout for Epic Records.

After appearing in the first season of *The Osbournes,* Jack also had the opportunity to act in other television programs, including *That '70s Show* and *Dawson's Creek.* He thoroughly enjoyed acting and was interested in doing more. "I had the best time. I don't know if this has sparked my acting career. We shall see." [84]

The Price of Fame

Although Jack Osbourne appreciated the opportunities which fame afforded him, he was skeptical about stardom. "I think the concept of fame is like a disease or one of those flesh-eating viruses. It starts in the finger and it will just spread. It's human nature to want a lot of attention." [85]

Like the rest of the family, Jack Osbourne was not prepared for the show's great success and popularity, or the degree of notoriety that he would receive. Sharon said that Jack had a very difficult time adjusting to the attention of the public and the press: "Jack was tearful every day. He didn't like being recognised with his mates, read unpleasant things on the internet, and thought he'd never be taken seriously." [86]

Jack Osbourne was also upset by the many stories about him in the press and the rumors showing up on the Internet. Several rumors started that he was homosexual, which he denied. "I'm not gay, although some viewers seem to think so. But I don't have a problem with homosexuality whatsoever." [87]

Additionally, Jack was sometimes hit or threatened because of his notoriety. He said: "A lot of people don't like me. I've been hit, I've been slapped in the face at a club and people drive by the house and scream that they're going to kick the hell out of me." [88]

New "Osbournes"

Nonetheless, Jack Osbourne, and the rest of the Osbournes, did their best to adapt to their increased celebrity status. In fact, Sharon Osbourne negotiated the family's return for a second season of the Osbournes, which began filming in summer 2002, for a reported sum of $39 million for twenty half-hour shows.

Among the noteworthy events covered by the second season was the addition of two new members of the Osbournes' extended family. In September 2002, Ozzy Osbourne discovered

The Osbournes welcomed Kelly's friend Robert Marcato (second from right) to the family in 2002.

that he had become a grandfather by his estranged first daughter, Jessica (Osbourne) Hobbs, who still lives in England; Ozzy Osbourne's granddaughter's name is Isabelle Hobbs.

Additionally, eighteen-year-old Robert Marcato, a longtime friend of Kelly Osbourne's from school, joined the Osbourne household after his mother, Reagan Marcato, a restaurant manager, died of colon cancer at age thirty-six on July 29, 2002. Sharon Osbourne had promised Reagan Marcato that the Osbourne family would provide a home for Robert and pay for his education. Ozzy Osbourne joked about Marcato living with them. He said, "One day he was just there. We're running a halfway house." [89]

Marcato moved into a guest house on the Osbourne's estate, behind the garden. As with their children, Ozzy and Sharon Osbourne have been generous with Marcato, giving him a Cadillac Escalade truck, and frequently giving him spending money.

The Osbournes got along well with their new family addition, and Sharon Osbourne said she had big plans for him: "We love [Robert] like he's our own. . . . I'm going to put that kid through drama school and he'll be the next Tom Cruise." [90]

Cancer

The summer of 2002 also provided the family with one of their greatest crises to date. On July 2, two days before Ozzy and Sharon Osbourne's twentieth wedding anniversary, Sharon Osbourne's doctor diagnosed her with colon cancer. The news shocked and frightened her:

> I mean, the first thing was fear. My stomach, like, was in knots. I couldn't breathe. I, I was hysterical. And the first thing you think of is, oh, my God. My kids, my kids. This can't be happening to me. You know, I'm not ready yet. It's not my time.[91]

Fortunately, Sharon Osbourne's doctors had caught the cancer early and were able to begin chemotherapy treatment immediately. Nonetheless, the rest of the Osbourne family, particularly Ozzy Osbourne, was very concerned about Sharon's health. Ozzy Osbourne said: "I'm not scared. I'm absolutely horrified. . . . It's the worst thing that can ever happen."[92]

Ozzy Osbourne was touring with Ozzfest 2002 at the time he received the news. He immediately cancelled his future performances so that he could be with his wife. He stayed home with Sharon and accompanied her to her chemotherapy treatments.

Feeling His Mortality

On April 10, 2001, Ozzy Osbourne's mother, Lillian Osbourne, died from complications from diabetes at age eighty-five. In her biography *Ozzy Unauthorized,* Sue Crawford describes Ozzy Osbourne's response.

> Although life on the road meant he had seen little of her for many years [Ozzy and his mother] had remained close. . . . Although she suffered from diabetes and kidney problems, he had been to see her a week earlier and she had seemed fine. If Ozzy had been devastated by the death of his father 23 years earlier, it was nothing compared to how he felt about losing his mother. Terrified that he might go to pieces completely, he decided not to attend the funeral. . . . "It might push me over the edge. I thought I was going nuts. . . . I was near the dark side. It was like waking up with the world's worst hangover, but I hadn't had a drink. I'm glued together with medications. I'm on everything—proper psychotic medication. If I don't pop pills I lose it."

However, the chemotherapy was almost as hard on him as it was on Sharon, and he fainted during her first treatment. After that, Sharon went on her own.

Ozzy Trying to Stay Sober

Sharon Osbourne said that her illness had been hard on everyone, but she was concerned about her husband because in the past he turned to alcohol during times of crisis. She said:

> Ozzy's trying really, really hard to stay sober, and it's really difficult for him right now. It's really difficult for anyone who's been an addict and an alcoholic their entire life, and, at the age of 54, he is still trying. . . . We try and make light of it: 'Oh, dad's an alcoholic, ha-ha-ha.' But it's a terrible thing when somebody's an alcoholic, because it's a disease and it's no different from me having cancer. It's a disease he can't help. He didn't start off in life saying 'I really want to be an addict and a[n] . . . alcoholic and spend my whole life in misery.'[93]

Sharon Osbourne knew that work was the best therapy for her husband, so she sent him back on tour with Ozzfest in August 2002. However, Ozzy Osbourne struggled while on the road, often sedating his frazzled nerves with beer. He said that it was difficult to perform as if Sharon were not sick:

> My heart was breaking every night onstage. I put on a brave face, but when you've got a broken heart 'cause somebody you love got sick, you can't pretend not to have a broken heart.[94]

An Osbourne Christmas

Sharon Osbourne responded well to her chemotherapy treatments, and by the end of 2002 the cancer had gone into remission and doctors expected her to make a complete recovery. Appreciative of the support of her family, friends, and fans, Sharon Osbourne made a television broadcast in Great Britain on Christmas Day to discuss the events of the year and express her gratitude. The program drew press coverage even before it was delivered because it was broadcast at the same time as Queen Elizabeth's traditional Christmas Day broadcast. Although the queen's broadcast beat out Sharon Osbourne's in the ratings, more than 4 million households tuned in to watch Sharon deliver her Christmas message.

In the broadcast, Sharon Osbourne expressed what she acknowledged as an uncharacteristically sentimental message to viewers: "It sounds kind of corny, but you know, kiss your mum, kiss your dad, kiss your brothers and your sisters, and you know, it's very important to love your family, especially at this time of year. . . . It's the one time that is so important that family are together and just give each other a big kiss."[95]

Still Crazy About Each Other

Ozzy and Sharon Osbourne also celebrated their good fortune and the positive prognosis for Sharon's health by renewing their wedding vows on December 31, 2002, in a ceremony at the Beverly Hills Hotel in Los Angeles. They had originally planned the event for July 4, 2002, which was their twentieth anniversary, but had postponed it because of Sharon's cancer diagnosis.

With daughter Kelly Osbourne acting as flower girl, and music provided by the '70s rock group the Village People, the reception lasted into the new year of 2003. Guests at the event included numerous celebrities, such as musician Justin Timberlake and comedian Chris Rock.

After being married to his wife for twenty years, Ozzy Osbourne said he and Sharon had a strong relationship built on love and frequent arguments. "I mean I always loved my wife but sometimes I don't like her and sometimes she doesn't like me. But we love each other. . . . I hate these people that go, 'Oh, we've been married 56 years and we've never had a bad word.' They must have been living on a different planet from each other."[96]

Into the Future

In early 2003, the Osbourne family looked back on the previous year with astonishment. The unexpected popularity of their television program, the opportunities and problems arising from it, and the family's personal crises and successes had made for an exciting and stressful year. According to Ozzy Osbourne, "This has been a pretty incredible year for the Osbournes, . . . both highs and lows."[97]

Both the highs and lows continued into 2003. For example, on April 23, Jack Osbourne checked into the Las Encinas Hospital in Pasedena to treat a drug and alcohol addiction that he had developed since *The Osbournes* began. "I got caught up in my new lifestyle and got carried away with drugs and alcohol," he said.

The love Ozzy and Sharon share for one another provides a solid foundation for their marriage and family.

"Once I realized this, I voluntarily checked myself into a detox facility for my own health and well-being." Ozzy Osbourne commended his son's bravery in admitting his addiction, saying "It takes a lot of courage to admit you need help, and both Sharon and I are proud Jack is facing his problems head on." [98]

Despite setbacks such as this, the Osbournes looked optimistically toward their future plans. A third season of *The Osbournes* is scheduled to air in June 2003; Kelly Osbourne bought her own multimillion dollar home only five blocks from her parents' house; Jack Osbourne looks forward to continuing his work as a talent scout and developing music producer; and Sharon Osbourne plans to start her own syndicated talk show in the fall of 2003. As for Ozzy Osbourne, his plans for the future are to return to business as usual: "I'm going to rock and roll." [99]

Notes

Introduction: Osbourne Family Values

1. Ed Masley, "Ozzy Osbourne Reaches a New Generation," *Chattanooga Times/Chattanooga Free Press,* August 9, 2002.
2. Quoted in Tony Hicks, "The Osbournes up Close," *Houston Chronicle,* May 7, 2002, p. 6.
3. Alessandra Stanley, "No Rest for Family Values on Black Sabbath," *New York Times,* April 2, 2002, p. E1.

Chapter 1: Ozzy: The Escape

4. Quoted in Garry Bushell, "I Was Really Worried About the Y2K Bug . . ." (Interview with Ozzy Osbourne), *Sun* (UK), April 28, 2001, p. 32
5. Quoted in Harry Shaw, *Ozzy "Talking": Ozzy Osbourne in His Own Words.* London: Omnibus Press, 2002, p. 8.
6. Quoted in Chris Nickson, *Ozzy Knows Best: An Unauthorized Biography.* New York: Thomas Dunne Books, 2002, p. 12.
7. Quoted in Jonathan Trew, "At His Satanic Majesty's Pleasure," *Scotland on Sunday,* May 19, 2002, p. 21.
8. Quoted in William Storr, "Interview: Ozzy Osbourne: Ozzy Rules," *Mirror* (UK), May 11, 2002, pp. 37–39.
9. Quoted in Shaw, *Ozzy "Talking,"* p. 14.
10. Quoted in the Osbournes with Todd Gold, *Officially Osbourne: Opening the Doors to the Land of Oz.* New York: MTV Books/ Pocket Books, 2002, p. 36.
11. Quoted in Shaw, *Ozzy "Talking,"* p. 11.

12. Quoted in Shaw, *Ozzy "Talking,"* p. 10.

13. Quoted in Jeb Brien, *Ozzy Osbourne: Don't Blame Me,* Sony Music Entertainment, 1991.

14. Quoted in Sue Crawford, *Ozzy Unauthorized.* London: Michael O'Mara Books, 2002 p. 39.

15. Quoted in Carol Clerk, *Diary of a Madman: Ozzy Osbourne: The Stories Behind the Songs.* New York: Thunder's Mouth Press, 2002, p. 13.

16. Quoted in Clerk, *Diary of a Madman,* p. 21.

17. Quoted in Storr, "Interview: Ozzy Osbourne," p. 37.

Chapter 2: Ozzy: Let the Madness Begin

18. Quoted in Crawford, *Ozzy Unauthorized,* p. 47.

19. Quoted in Amanda Craig, "Mad, Bad and the Teenager's Perfect Dad," *Sunday Times* (London), April 21, 2002.

20. Quoted in Charlotte Ward, "Now and Then . . . Ozzy Osbourne on Stage at the Jubilee in Buckingham," *Sunday Mercury* (UK), June 9, 2002, p. 16.

21. Quoted in Oliver Harvey, "I Can't Believe I've Been Invited to Buckingham Palace," *Sun* (UK), May 25, 2002, p. 36.

22. Quoted in Garry Bushell, "My 22 Years of Madness & Mayhem with Wild Man Ozzy; Inside the Mad, Mad World of Wildest Rocker on the Planet," *People* (UK), June 16, 2002, p. 31.

23. Quoted in Crawford, *Ozzy Unauthorized,* p. 64.

24. Quoted in Shaw, *Ozzy "Talking,"* p. 42.

25. Quoted in Nickson, *Ozzy Knows Best,* p. 41.

26. Quoted in Shaw, *Ozzy "Talking,"* p. 10.

27. Quoted in Brien, *Ozzy Osbourne.*

28. Quoted in Shaw, *Ozzy "Talking,"* p. 43.

29. Quoted in Montgomery Brower, "Life with Ozzy Osbourne, Says His Wife, Sharon, Is a Heavy Test of Mettle," *People Weekly,* July 10, 1989, p. 94.

30. Quoted in Sue Crawford, "Ozzy's Iron Maiden," *Sunday Telegraph Magazine* (Sydney), July 28, 2002, p. Z04.

31. Quoted in *People in the News*, "Profiles of Ozzy Osbourne, Elvis Costello, David Bowie, Norah Jones," CNN, November 30, 2002.
32. Quoted in David Thomas, "The Woman Who Tamed Ozzy," *Sunday Telegraph* (London), May 19, 2002, p. 03.

Chapter 3: Ozzy and Sharon: Starting Over

33. Quoted in Crawford, *Ozzy Unauthorized*, p. 93.
34. Quoted in Crawford, *Ozzy Unauthorized*, p. 94.
35. Quoted in CNN, *People in the News*.
36. Quoted in Nickson, *Ozzy Knows Best*, p. 60.
37. Quoted in Brien, *Ozzy Osbourne*.
38. Quoted in CNN, *People in the News*.
39. Quoted in Shaw, *Ozzy "Talking,"* p. 52.
40. Quoted in David Thomas, "Sharon's Nights of Terror: Sharon Osbourne Suffered Ozzy's Violence Until She Found Her Strength," *Vancouver Province*, June 23, 2002, p. B5.
41. Quoted in Crawford, "Ozzy's Iron Maiden," p. 4.
42. Quoted in Brower, "Life with Ozzy Osbourne, p. 94.
43. Quoted in Brower, "Life with Ozzy Osbourne, p. 94.
44. Quoted in *Rolling Stone*, "Women in Rock: Sharon Osbourne," October 31, 2002, p. 54.

Chapter 4: Ozzy and Sharon: Working Through It

45. Quoted in Michael Small, "Chatter (Ozzy Osbourne)," *People Weekly*, February 18, 1985, p. 114.
46. Quoted in *Toronto Star*, "Suicide Victim's Father Sues Rock Singer," January 14, 1986.
47. Quoted in Michael Lalonde, "The Complete Ozzy Osbourne Biography," www.geocities.com.
48. Clerk, *Diary of a Madman*, p. 97.
49. Quoted in Mick Brown, "Biting Comments Test Ozzy's Metal; Ozzy Osbourne," *Times* (London), May 29, 1988.
50. Quoted in Brien, *Ozzy Osbourne*.
51. Quoted in Brien, *Ozzy Osbourne*.

52. Quoted in Thomas, "Sharon's Nights of Terror," p. B5.

53. Quoted in Crawford, "Ozzy's Iron Maiden," p. 4.

54. Quoted in Crawford, "Ozzy's Iron Maiden," p. 4.

55. Quoted in Storr, "Interview: Ozzy Osbourne," p. 37.

56. Quoted in Thomas, "The Woman Who Tamed Ozzy," p. 03.

57. Quoted in *People in the News,* "Interviews with Paula Zahn, Sharon Collins, Mark Viviano, Gail O'Neill," CNN, May 11, 2002.

58. Quoted in Brien, *Ozzy Osbourne.*

59. Quoted in Deborah Russell, "Ozzy Osbourne's 'Tears' of Satisfaction: Says His 'Madman' Persona Ends with Album," *Billboard,* October 12, 1991, p. 32.

60. Quoted in Clerk, *Diary of a Madman,* p. 132.

61. Quoted in Kelly Barbieri, "Hard Music: The Blizzard of Ozz," *Billboard,* June 29, 2002, p. 21.

62. Quoted in Nancy Miller, "Iron Maiden," *Entertainment Weekly,* September 1, 2000, p. 24.

63. Quoted in *Memphis Commercial Appeal,* "Osbourne Faces Down His Demons but 'Merry Mayhem' Still Rocks," November 2, 2001, p. G2.

64. Quoted in *Memphis Commercial Appeal,* "Osbourne Faces Down His Demons But 'Merry Mayhem' Still Rocks," p. G2.

65. Quoted in Harvey, "I Can't Believe I've Been Invited to Buckingham Palace," p. 36.

Chapter 5: MTV's First Family

66. Ozzy and Sharon Osbourne, *Fox on the Record with Greta Van Susteren,* July 5, 2002.

67. Ozzy and Sharon Osbourne, *Fox on the Record with Greta Van Susteren.*

68. Quoted in the Osbournes with Gold, *Officially Osbourne,* p. 75.

69. Quoted in MSN, "Chat with the Osbournes," May 7, 2002.

70. Quoted in Harvey, "I Can't Believe I've Been Invited to Buckingham Palace," p. 36.

71. Quoted in Andrew Duncan, "Mad and Bad in Beverly Hills," *Radio Times,* October 26, 2002, p. 16.

72. Quoted in Phil Rosenthal, "Sharon's Crazy Train of Thought," *Chicago Sun-Times,* November 5, 2002, p. 37.

73. Quoted in Edna Gunderson, "Uncovering the Real Osbournes," *USA Today,* November 22, 2002, p. 1E.

74. Quoted in David Keeps, "Osbourne to Be Wild," *Teen People,* November 2002, p. 96.

75. Quoted in MSN, "Chat with the Osbournes."

76. Quoted in Dominic Mohan, "I'm a Bad Drinker . . . I Didn't Inherit That Ozzy Gene," *Sun* (UK), August 23, 2002, p. 36.

77. Quoted in Jenny Eliscu, "*Rolling Stone*'s People of the Year: Kelly Osbourne," *Rolling Stone,* December 12, 2002, p. 76.

78. Quoted in Ann Haley, "You Say It's Your Birthday? That's Some Surpise Gift," *Orange County Register,* February 24, 2003.

79. Quoted in Jenny Johnston, "Kelly Osbourne on Being Dumped," *Mirror.* www.mirror.co.uk.

80. Leigh Mytton, "Osbourne Tackles Teen Angst," BBC News Online, February 14, 2003. http://news.bbc.co.uk.

81. Maddy Costa, "Kelly Osbourne, Shut Up," *The Guardian* (UK), February 7, 2003.

82. Quoted in Keeps, "Osbourne to Be Wild," p. 96.

83. Quoted in Tom Beaujour, "You Don't Know Jack," *New York Times Magazine,* November 24, 2002.

84. Quoted in Keeps, "Osbourne to Be Wild," p. 96.

85. Quoted in Beaujour, "You Don't Know Jack," p. 622.

86. Quoted in Duncan, "Mad and Bad in Beverly Hills," p. 16.

87. Quoted in Michael Lewittes, "Osbourne: Ladies' Man," *Us Weekly,* May 20, 2002, p. 6.

88. Quoted in Beaujour, "You Don't Know Jack," p. 622.

89. Quoted in Gunderson, "Uncovering the Real Osbournes," p. 1E.

90. Quoted in Keeps, "Osbourne to Be Wild," p. 96.

91. Sharon Osbourne, interview with Barbara Walters, *Good Morning America,* ABC, November 6, 2002.

92. Quoted in Osbourne, interview with Walters, *Good Morning America.*

93. Quoted in Christopher Goodwin, "They're No Joke," *Sunday Times* (London), October 26, 2002, p. Features; Culture; 6.

94. Quoted in Caryn James, "The Osbournes Return Still Weird and Warm," *New York Times,* November 26, 2002, p. 1.

95. Quoted in TCM Breaking News, "Sharon Osbourne in Ratings Battle with the Queen," December 23, 2002.

96. Quoted in CNN, *People in the News.*

97. Quoted in Tom Gilatto and Alexis Chiu, "Daze of Their Lives," *People Weekly,* December 9, 2002, p. 66.

98. Quoted in "Jack Osbourne Reportedly in Rehab For Drug Abuse," Associated Press, April 30, 2003.

99. Quoted in CNBC, "Business Center," March 18, 2002.

Important Dates in the Lives of the Osbournes

December 3, 1948
John Michael "Ozzy" Osbourne is born.

October 9, 1952
Sharon Arden is born.

1967
Ozzy Osbourne, Tony Iommi, Geezer Butler, and Bill Ward form Earth.

1968
Earth changes their name to Black Sabbath.

February 13, 1970
Black Sabbath's self-titled debut album is released on Vertigo Records in the UK.

1971
Ozzy Osbourne marries Birmingham girlfriend Thelma Mayfair.

1972
Ozzy and Thelma Osbourne's daughter Jessica Starshine is born.

1975
Ozzy and Thelma Osbourne's son Louis is born.

January 20, 1978
Ozzy's father, John "Jack" Osbourne, Sr. dies.

1979
Ozzy is fired from Black Sabbath and spends months locked in hotel room bingeing on drugs and alcohol. Sharon Arden cleans him up and persuades him to form a solo band.

September 1980
Ozzy Osbourne's first solo album, *Blizzard of Ozz,* is released in the UK.

1981
Blizzard of Ozz is released in the United States. Ozzy and Thelma Osbourne divorce.

July 4, 1982
Ozzy Osbourne and Sharon Arden marry in Maui.

November 1982
Ozzy and Sharon Osbourne break away from the management of Don Arden, beginning a nineteen-year feud between Don Arden and Sharon Osbourne.

September 2, 1983
Aimee Rachel Osbourne is born.

December 31, 1983
On New Year's Eve, James Jollimore murders three people after listening to Ozzy Osbourne's album *Bark at the Moon.*

October 27, 1984
Ozzy and Sharon Osbourne's second daughter, Kelly Lee Osbourne, is born.

November 8, 1985
Ozzy and Sharon Osbourne's third child, Jack Osbourne, is born.

August 1989
Ozzy Osbourne plays the Moscow Music Peace Festival in Russia.

September 1989
Ozzy Osbourne is arrested for the attempted murder of Sharon Osbourne.

September 1996
The first Ozzfest is held in Phoenix and in Los Angeles.

April 10, 2001
Ozzy's mother, Lillian Osbourne, dies.

March 2002
The Osbournes premieres on MTV to immediate success.

April 2002
Ozzy Osbourne receives a star on Hollywood's Walk of Fame.

May 2002

Ozzy and Sharon Osbourne attend a press dinner with President Bush at the White House.

June 2002

Ozzy Osbourne sings for Queen Elizabeth II in her garden at Buckingham Palace as part of her Golden Jubilee.

July 2002

Sharon Osbourne is diagnosed with colon cancer.

November 2002

Kelly Osbourne's debut album, *Shut Up*, is released.

November 26, 2002

The second season of *The Osbournes* airs.

December 31, 2002

Ozzy and Sharon Osbourne renew their wedding vows.

February 2003

Kelly Osbourne tours for her debut album, *Shut Up*.

For Further Reading

Books

The Osbournes with Todd Gold, *Officially Osbourne: Opening the Doors to the Land of Oz.* New York: MTV Books/Pocket Books, 2002. An authorized biography of the Osbourne family, including brief profiles of each family member and lengthy synopses of and supplementary information about *The Osbournes* television program's first season. Includes extensive color photos and artwork.

Reed Tucker, *The Osbournes UnFxxxingAuthorized: The Completely Unauthorized and Unofficial Guide to Everything Osbourne.* New York: Bantam Books, 2002. Very brief biography of the Osbourne family. Focuses on plot synopses of *The Osbournes* television program's first season. Includes color photos and Osbourne trivia.

Video

Jeb Brien, *Ozzy Osbourne: Don't Blame Me.* Sony Music Entertainment, 1991. Video biography of Ozzy Osbourne, focusing on his career and personal life from 1968 to 1991. Includes extensive Osbourne interview footage from over the years, with numerous commentaries from others that knew or were influenced by Osbourne.

Websites

MTV on Air: The Osbournes (www.mtv.com). The official MTV network website for *The Osbournes.* Includes episode guides for the television program; brief biographies of the Osbourne family members and their staff; photos; games; and trivia.

Kelly Osbourne (http://kellyosbourne.com). A website with regularly updated news regarding Kelly Osbourne and her career. Includes brief biography of the artist, message boards, wallpaper downloads, and dates of upcoming appearances.

Ozzy (www.ozzy.com). A website with frequently updated news on Ozzy Osbourne and *The Osbournes*.

Works Consulted

Books

Carol Clerk, *Diary of a Madman: Ozzy Osbourne: The Stories Behind the Songs*. New York: Thunder's Mouth Press, 2002. This volume combines biographical information about Osbourne's childhood and his full career, through his years with Black Sabbath, *Blizzard of Ozz*, his solo career, and the MTV program *The Osbournes*. It focuses on anecdotes and biographical details that influenced or inspired Black Sabbath and solo songs. Contains numerous color photographs, timeline, and discography.

Sue Crawford, *Ozzy Unauthorized*. London: Michael O'Mara Books, 2002. Good biography that includes details from Ozzy Osbourne's life not found in other books or articles. Includes numerous color photographs and extensive discography.

David Katz and Michael Robin, *The Osbournes: The Unauthorized !@#$-ing True Story of the Osbourne Family*. Kansas City: Roundtable Press, 2002. Brief biography dealing with the entire Osbourne family, their staff, friends, and pets. Includes many color photos.

Chris Nickson, *Ozzy Knows Best: An Unauthorized Biography*. New York: Thomas Dunne Books, 2002. This biography covers Osbourne's life and career from childhood through the end of *The Osbournes* television program's first season, as well as biographical information about Sharon, Kelly, and Jack Osbourne. Derived from secondary sources and including sidebars with Osbourne "factoids" and trivia, the book is a useful source. Contains a few black-and-white photos.

Harry Shaw, *Ozzy "Talking": Ozzy Osbourne in His Own Words*. London: Omnibus Press, 2002. A useful collection of quotations by Osbourne gathered from interviews and articles, commenting on his biography and career. Explicit language intact. Contains numerous photos, in black-and-white and in color.

Periodicals

Kelly Barbieri, "Hard Music: The Blizzard of Ozz," *Billboard*, June 29, 2002.

Tom Beaujour, "You Don't Know Jack," *New York Times Magazine*, November 24, 2002.

Montgomery Brower, "Life with Ozzy Osbourne, Says His Wife, Sharon, Is a Heavy Test of Mettle," *People Weekly*, July 10, 1989.

Elizabeth F. Brown and William R. Hendee, "Adolescents and Their Music: Insights into the Health of Adolescents," *JAMA*, Sept 22, 1989.

Mick Brown, "Biting Comments Test Ozzy's Metal; Ozzy Osbourne," *Times* (London), May 29, 1988.

Garry Bushell, "I Was Really Worried about the Y2K Bug . . ." (Interview with Ozzy Osbourne), *Sun* (UK), April 28, 2001.

Garry Bushell, "My 22 Years of Madness & Mayhem with Wild Man Ozzy; Inside the Mad, Mad World of Wildest Rocker on the Planet," *People* (UK), June 16, 2002.

CNBC, "Business Center," March 18, 2002.

Maddy Costa, "Kelly Osbourne, Shut Up," *Guardian* (UK), February 7, 2003.

Paul Cotton, "Medium Isn't Accurate 'Ice Age' Message," *JAMA*, May 23, 1990.

Claire Cozens, "MTV Staged Key Scenes of Osbournes, Claim Stars," *Guardian*, November 27, 2002.

Amanda Craig, "Mad, Bad and the Teenager's Perfect Dad," *Sunday Times* (London), April 21, 2002.

Sue Crawford, "Ozzy's Iron Maiden," *Sunday Telegraph Magazine* (Sydney), July 28, 2002.

Andrew Duncan, "Mad and Bad in Beverly Hills," *Radio Times,* October 26, 2002.

Jenny Eliscu, "*Rolling Stone*'s People of the Year: Kelly Osbourne," *Rolling Stone,* December 12, 2002.

Tom Gilatto and Alexis Chiu, "The Daze of Their Lives," *People Weekly,* December 9, 2002.

Ian Gittins, "The Friday Interview: Eminem Sings About Killing His Wife. My Husband Actually Tried to Do It: Sharon Osbourne Tells Ian Gittens How She Took a Booze-Soaked Rock 'n' Roll Has-Been and Turned Him into a 40M Pounds Industry," *Guardian,* May 25, 2001.

Christopher Goodwin, "They're No Joke," *Sunday Times* (London), October 26, 2002.

Kieran Grant, "Diary of a Madman; Black Sabbath's Ozzy Osbourne Has Left a Trail of Tales—Some Real, Some Imagined," *Toronto Sun,* July 22, 2001.

Ann Haley, "You Say It's Your Birthday? That's Some Surpise Gift," *Orange County Register,* February 24, 2003.

Oliver Harvey, "I Can't Believe I've Been Invited to Buckingham Palace . . . ," *Sun* (UK), May 25, 2002.

Chris Heath, "The Most Loved and Feared Woman in the Music Business on How She Got to Be That Way," *Rolling Stone,* October 31, 2002.

Erik Hedegaard, "Ozzy Osbourne: Out of the Box," *Scotsman* (Scotland), August 3, 2002.

Tony Hicks, "The Osbournes up Close," *Houston Chronicle,* May 7, 2002.

"Jack Osbourne Reportedly in Rehab for Drug Abuse," Associated Press, April 30, 2003.

Caryn James, "The Osbournes Return Still Weird and Warm," *New York Times,* November 26, 2002.

David Keeps, "Osbourne to Be Wild," *Teen People,* November 2002.

"Kelly Osbourne Reflects on TV Show Image," Associated Press, March 4, 2003.

Taylor Kingston, "Under the Influence of Heavy Metal," *St. Louis Post-Dispatch,* March 17, 1990.

Michael Lewittes, "Osbourne: Ladies' Man," *Us Weekly,* May 20, 2002.

Ed Masley, "Ozzy Osbourne Reaches a New Generation," *Chattanooga Times/Chattanooga Free Press,* August 9, 2002.

Memphis Commercial Appeal, "Osbourne Faces Down His Demons but 'Merry Mayhem' Still Rocks," November 2, 2001.

Nancy Miller, "Iron Maiden," *Entertainment Weekly,* September 1, 2000.

Elvis Mitchell, "Kelly & Jack Osbourne: Osbourne Gave Birth to Heavy Metal. But His Other Offspring Gave MTV Its Biggest Hit Ever—And New Life to His Career," *Interview,* June, 2002.

Dominic Mohan, "I'm A Bad Drinker . . . I Didn't Inherit That Ozzy Gene," *Sun* (UK), August 23, 2002.

MSN, "Chat with the Osbournes," May 7, 2002.

Kim Neely, "Ozzy Osbourne," *Rolling Stone,* September 30, 1993.

Ozzy Osbourne, interview with Rod Black and Lisa LaFlamme, *Canada AM,* CTV Television, July 1, 2002.

Ozzy and Sharon Osbourne, *Fox on the Record with Greta Van Susteren,* Fox News, May 27, 2002.

Sharon Osbourne, interview with Barbara Walters, *Good Morning America,* ABC, November 6, 2002.

People in the News, "Headline: Profiles of Madonna, Ozzy Osbourne, Natalie Portman," CNN, May 11, 2002.

People in the News, "Headline: Profiles of Ozzy Osbourne, Elvis Costello, David Bowie, Norah Jones," CNN, November 30, 2002.

People Weekly, "The 50 Most Beautiful People: Sharon Osbourne," May 13, 2002.

Jim Pfiffer, "Cardinal: 2 Exorcisms Performed in New York," *USA Today,* March 6, 1990.

Rolling Stone, "Women in Rock: Sharon Osbourne," October 31, 2002.

Phil Rosenthal, "Sharon's Crazy Train of Thought," *Chicago Sun-Times,* November 5, 2002.

Deborah Russell, "Ozzy Osbourne's 'Tears' of Satisfaction: Says His 'Madman' Persona Ends with Album," *Billboard*, October 12, 1991.

Michael Small, "Chatter (Ozzy Osbourne)," *People Weekly*, February 18, 1985.

Alessandra Stanley, "No Rest for Family Values on Black Sabbath," *New York Times*, April 2, 2002.

St. Louis Post-Dispatch, "Noisome? Cardinal Links Rock, Demonic Possession," March 7, 1990.

St. Louis Post-Dispatch, "People Column," March 7, 1990.

William Storr, "Ozzy Osbourne: Ozzy Rules," *Mirror* (UK), May 11, 2002.

TCM Breaking News, "Sharon Osbourne in Ratings Battle with the Queen," December 23, 2002.

David Thomas, "Sharon's Nights of Terror: Sharon Osbourne Suffered Ozzy's Violence Until She Found Her Strength," *Vancouver Province*, June 23, 2002.

David Thomas, "The Woman Who Tamed Ozzy," *Sunday Telegraph* (London), May 19, 2002.

Toronto Star, "Suicide Victim's Father Sues Rock Singer," January 14, 1986.

Jonathan Trew, "At His Satanic Majesty's Pleasure," *Scotland on Sunday*, May 19, 2002.

Charlotte Ward, "Now and Then . . . Ozzy Osbourne on Stage at the Jubilee in Buckingham," *Sunday Mercury* (UK), June 9, 2002.

John Widerhorn, "Ozzy Osbourne," *Rolling Stone*, June 26, 1997.

Videos

Black Sabbath Story, vol. 1 (1970–1978). Castle Communications, Time-Warner Video, 1991. A video anthology of the biggest hits of the early years of Black Sabbath, when Ozzy Osbourne was a member of the band. This video provides only a little information about the band. Rather, it focuses on several significant performances by the band.

Jeb Brien, *Ozzy Osbourne: Don't Blame Me*. Sony Music Entertainment, 1991. A documentary of the first twenty-three years of Ozzy

Osbourne's career. This video includes numerous interviews with Ozzy and Sharon Osbourne, as well as those with friends and associates of Ozzy Osbourne. The film focuses on Osbourne's off-stage life and personality to provide a better understanding of the man behind the many rumors and controversies that have surrounded his career.

Internet Sources

"Aimee Osbourne Set to Hit Big Time," February 10, 2003. www.teen music.com.

Edna Gunderson, "Uncovering the Real Osbournes," *USA Today,* November 22, 2002. www.usatoday.com.

Jenny Johnston, "Kelly Osbourne on Being Dumped," *Mirror.* www. mirror.co.uk

"Kelly Osbourne to Star in Doritos Ad," Breaking News, March 6, 2003. www.breakingnews.ie.

Michael Lalonde, "The Complete Ozzy Osbourne Biography." www.geocities.com.

Leigh Mytton, "Osbourne Tackles Teen Angst," BBC News Online, February 14, 2003. http://news.bbc.co.uk.

"Ozzy Needs Medical Help for Tour Sobriety," March 8, 2003. www.teenmusic.com.

Chris Pursell, "Tribune After Ma Osbourne," *TV Week,* December 16, 2002. www.tvweek.com.

Website

The Complete Ozzy Osbourne Biography (www.faqs.org). A text-only, detailed biography of Ozzy Osbourne, assembled from numerous sources and frequently updated.

Index

Picture Credits

About the Author

Andy Koopmans's other books include biographies on Bruce Lee, Madonna, and Charles Lindbergh. He is also the author of *Understanding Great Literature: Lord of the Flies* and the editor of *Examining Popular Culture: Crime and Criminals*. His fiction, poetry, reviews, and essays have been published in a variety of journals and magazines.

He lives in Seattle with his wife Angela Mihm, their cats Bubz and Licorice, and their faithful wonderdog Zachary.

He would like to thank the staff at Lucent Books, particularly Jennifer Skancke, for their assistance in preparing this manuscript for publication.